HOW TO SAY IT

Be Indispensable at Work

HOW TO SAY IT

Be Indispensable at Work

Winning Words and Strategies to
Get Noticed, Get Hired, and Get Ahead

JACK GRIFFIN

Prentice Hall Press

PRENTICE HALL PRESS
Published by the Penguin Group
Penguin Group (USA) Inc.
375 Hudson Street, New York, New York 10014, USA
Penguin Group (Canada), 90 Eglinton Avenue East, Suite 700, Toronto, Ontario M4P 2Y3, Canada
(a division of Pearson Penguin Canada Inc.)
Penguin Books Ltd., 80 Strand, London WC2R 0RL, England
Penguin Group Ireland, 25 St. Stephen's Green, Dublin 2, Ireland (a division of Penguin Books Ltd.)
Penguin Group (Australia), 250 Camberwell Road, Camberwell, Victoria 3124, Australia
(a division of Pearson Australia Group Pty. Ltd.)
Penguin Books India Pvt. Ltd., 11 Community Centre, Panchsheel Park, New Delhi—110 017, India
Penguin Group (NZ), 67 Apollo Drive, Rosedale, North Shore 0632, New Zealand
(a division of Pearson New Zealand Ltd.)
Penguin Books (South Africa) (Pty.) Ltd., 24 Sturdee Avenue, Rosebank, Johannesburg 2196,
South Africa

Penguin Books Ltd., Registered Offices: 80 Strand, London WC2R 0RL, England

While the author has made every effort to provide accurate telephone numbers and Internet addresses at
the time of publication, neither the publisher nor the author assumes any responsibility for errors or for
changes that occur after publication. Further, the publisher does not have any control over and does not
assume any responsibility for author or third-party websites or their content.

First edition: April 2011

Library of Congress Cataloging-in-Publication Data

Griffin, Jack.
  How to say it : be indispensable at work : winning words and strategies to get noticed, get hired, and
get ahead / Jack Griffin.— 1st ed.
    p. cm.
  Includes index.
  ISBN 978-0-7352-0454-6
  1. Business communication. 2. Communication in organizations. 3. Oral communication. I. Title.
  HF5718.G7482   2011
  650.1′3—dc22   2010046854

PRINTED IN THE UNITED STATES OF AMERICA

10 9 8 7 6 5 4 3 2 1

Most Prentice Hall Press books are available at special quantity discounts for bulk purchases for sales
promotions, premiums, fund-raising, or educational use. Special books, or book excerpts, can also be
created to fit specific needs. For details, write: Special Markets, Penguin Group (USA) Inc., 375 Hudson
Street, New York, New York 10014.

As ever, for Flora

ACKNOWLEDGMENTS

Many thanks to my editor, Maria Gagliano, who showed me how to get this book to end up much better than it started out.

CONTENTS

Part Three: Holding On and Breaking Through

PREFACE

Irreplaceable, Indispensable, Incredible You

Times are tough.

The phrase is so true it's tired, and I'm tired of it. This book will help you be one of the millions who work when others aren't working. But it's about much more than surviving tough times. It's about building—a career, a future, a set of alternatives. This is a book about not only *making* yourself irreplaceable and indispensable in your workplace and in your industry, but *branding* yourself in this way to your boss, your coworkers, your staff, and to yourself. It's about finding the fire in your belly and about marketing your skills, competencies, achievements, and potential not just to a prospective employer, but to your present employer.

How to Say It: Be Indispensable at Work is not full of feel-good mantras and it's not a new theory of management. It's a compact, concise, hard-nosed set of strategies and words that will get you hired, get you noticed, and get you ahead—because staying employed is always important, but it's never enough.

Finding Facts and Facing Facts

In any enterprise, bad information is an enemy, good information an ally. Part One is all about getting the good stuff, the information that will help you make yourself irreplaceable, indispensable, and incredible to those you work with and work for. Chapter 1 provides the tools you need to accurately assess the state of your workplace, your company, and your industry now. After you accurately assess workplace, company, and industry, Chapter 2 will show you how to take a frank, unblinking inventory of your achievements and your transferable skills—the elements of your personal human capital: the basic "value proposition" you offer your employer. Chapter 3 will take you beyond the basic self-assessment of Chapter 2 and show you how to dig for your "buried treasure"—the powerful elements within you that you have yet to exploit, perhaps have yet to discover. Finally, armed with an assessment of your working environment and all that you have to offer, the last chapter in Part One guides you in setting goals that are as high as your dreams can set them—even in (*especially in*) a challenging economy.

CHAPTER 1

REALITY CHECK

Tough times. Lean times. Hard times. Scary times. Doesn't really matter what you call the particular year, quarter, month, day, or minute you happen to occupy. If you're in a job that offers a living wage—or something even better—you are always working in highly competitive times. This is the case whether the economy is going bust or going gangbusters. The facts, eternal and immutable, are these: Your employer wants problems solved, opportunities exploited, the job done. Convince your boss that no one solves, exploits, and does more and better than you, and you will make yourself indispensable. Not only does that mean you'll keep your job but also it will clear the way for more of a job—more responsibility, more money, and more of a future, for the simple reason that your boss and her bosses will want more of you. In tough times? *Especially* in tough times.

Read the Writing on the Wall
(Before They Knock the Walls Down)

This book is about rising even when the times seem to be all about falling. The best way to hold on to your job is to make yourself indispensable in it, which means doing everything possible to make your bosses want not only to keep you but to give you more.

But before you can rise, you need to know if the ground is firm beneath you.

You cannot know where to go, much less how to get there, unless you first determine, realistically, where you and your firm stand.

Sometimes, the first word you hear of a downsizing, business closure, mass layoff, or a layoff targeting just you is shortly before it happens or even when it happens. Sometimes, management will be open, honest, transparent, and give you fair warning. Sometimes. More often, it's up to you to read the handwriting on the wall. Here are seven signs that your company—and therefore your job—may be in trouble:

1. **The star players are leaving. The back-benchers are staying.** If you notice that the best people, the movers and the shakers, the folks you (and others) admire most are jumping ship, take the hint. Not only is this a probable sign of a troubled company, it can readily make a troubled situation more troubled. The best two or three people leaving is like the first rocks in a landslide. Their loss can trigger an avalanche. Really good employees like to work alongside other really good people. The loss of more than a few of these tends to trigger the flight of even more. In contrast, the less able, the back-bench players, tend to stick around, and if they're in a position of power, they are also inclined to hire and promote other also-rans

or, worse, people incapable of even finishing the race. In this way, the cracks in a company's foundation may broaden into a full-scale collapse.

2. **The company stops making sense to you.** If you find that you can no longer understand your company's strategy, don't be too quick to sell yourself short by assuming management is just too clever for you. The fact is that viable companies formulate strategies that make sense and that are essentially straightforward and pretty easy to understand. The strategy of a good company can be explained concisely and clearly without obscure language, imprecise verbiage, or a lot of weasel words. If you cannot understand your company's strategy and, equally important, cannot explain that strategy to others, your company is likely headed for a fall.

3. **The company lags behind the rest of the industry.** Market-leading companies are called "market-leading" because they lead, rather than follow, the market. They grow faster than their market does. This is how a successful company expands sales while it simultaneously grabs market share from its competitors. If you (or others in the company or the company as a whole) are losing sales while the industry is doing well, your company is faltering.

4. **Off the mark time and again.** Few firms hit their target numbers every time, especially when the economy is "challenging." But when missing the target becomes routine (in a public company, falling short of quarterly Wall Street earnings; in a privately held firm, failing to achieve internal budget goals), something more than a tough economy is happening.

5. **The layoff parade marches on—and on.** In tough times, with demand contracting, companies lay people off. It's a hard fact of life.

But when layoffs are repeated, becoming almost routine, you know there's trouble.

6. **Cash-flow problems.** Look into your company's cash position— something that's easier to do in a publicly traded company than in one that's privately or closely held. If more cash consistently goes out than comes in, you are approaching the End Time. Like Grandpa used to say, "Taking out without putting in soon hits bottom."

7. **Nobody's sayin' nuthin'.** When management stops communicating meaningfully with you and your colleagues, you probably should assume the worst. Failure to communicate is not synonymous with silence. Words are supposed to reveal, not conceal. If you cannot understand what management is saying to you—if it's all jargon, double-speak, and technobabble—suspect that there is something to hide.

Seeing the Bull's-eye on Your Back

Sometimes the ship you're on starts sinking, and sometimes you get thrown overboard. Again, the first indication that you are being targeted for removal may be a frank, straightforward conversation with your boss, but, more often, rumblings can be heard well before you are made to walk the plank. Listen for them and know how to interpret them:

1. **You've lost *your* boss.** For whatever reason, your boss or mentor has moved on or moved out, and the new guy doesn't like you or the work you're doing. As far as you can tell, *his* bosses love him. There could be trouble ahead, especially if the new guy has an entourage he's itching to bring in.

2. **You lose the space race.** You had an office with four walls and a door, and now you're being asked to move to a cube; or you're the only person at your level who's still in a cube; or everyone's in a cube, but your cube's been moved to the basement. This is the corporate equivalent of the bum's rush. Back in the day when men wore hats, someone who wanted you to go would hand you your hat, smile, and say, "Here's your hat. What's your hurry?"

3. **Your boss starts a paper trail behind you.** If your bosses suddenly start putting everything in writing that used to be conveyed in a friendly chat, there's reason to believe that a paper trail is being blazed to satisfy HR preparatory to termination.

4. **You find yourself out of the loop.** Memos fly past you, meetings are held without you. The "freeze out" is always a bad sign.

5. **You're given the short end.** Lately, all the dead-end scut work assignments have been heaped on you; or you're being assigned missions doomed to fail. You feel you're being deliberately set up to look bad.

6. **Your company's been merged or sold.** Mergers and sales almost always create real or perceived "redundancies" and therefore bring layoffs. If your company's on the block, get ready to move or be moved: *out*.

Getting Good Information

If you decide that you have good reason to believe that your job is in danger, talk to your boss. An obvious step? Yes. And you didn't need this book to tell you to take it. But read on. While this is an *obvious* step, it is *not* the first step you should take.

Think about it. You've already spoken to management at least once about your employment situation. Remember? It was called a *job interview.* Now, maybe you didn't bone up for that interview, just winged it, got lucky, and got the job. Chances are, however, that you prepared. At the very least, you probably took time to find out something about the company's business, so that when the interviewer asked you if you had any questions, you didn't reply with "Yeah, what is it you guys do anyway?" More likely, you dug into the firm's website, maybe looked the company up in trade and other publications, asked colleagues about it, did a Google or other web search, found out something about competitors and the industry generally, and so on. You understood that, while job interviewers appreciate your questions, what they're really looking for is answers. So—probably—you went into the interview armed with at least some answers.

Talking to your boss about your future with the department or the company is a job interview. This is true any time you talk to her, but it is especially critical in hard times. Don't walk into the conversation cold. Don't walk into it with nothing but questions. Prepare yourself with information. Prepare yourself with answers. Remember, whatever else your boss wants from you—a particular skill, a particular attitude, a particular set of qualifications—what she most wants is for you to solve the problems she has, not create fresh problems for her.

About Your Company

Start with what is closest to you. Go through your email inbox for the latest company and departmental memos and newsletters—you know, the stuff that comes in on a daily or weekly basis and that you never get around to reading. Well, read this material now.

Next, review the basics—the kind of documents you would pore over if you were interviewing for the job you already happen to have:

- **Review your job description.** Make sure you know what you contribute to the enterprise. Underscore the active and affirmative aspects of your job. Show how what you do matters to the company.

- **Review any recent performance evaluations.** Take note of the good, the bad, and the ugly. Be prepared to trumpet the good and to address—proactively and positively—the bad and the ugly.

- **Take a look at your firm's website.** Look at the tab that says "About Us." Read it. If there is a tab that provides access to press releases, click on it. Look at the most recent stories. Watch for significant issues: "Acme Industries CEO Sees Tough Times Ahead," "Acme Industries in Merger Talks with XYZ," "Acme to Scale Back Widget Division," and the like. Look for "In the News" or "Acme in the News," and be sure to click on "From the CEO." Then go to "Investor Relations" or "For Investors" or "Annual Report." Read all of this material before you even *think* of asking your boss, "How am I doing?"

- **Scour the media for mentions of your firm.** Do a Google or other web search, using your company's name as keyword. If your company subscribes to industry publications, be sure to scan through these.

- **Access sales figures.** Do *not* attempt to access information for which you do not have authorization. You don't need to break into the vault or rifle through confidential files, but do gather whatever performance data is legitimately available to you. Depending on your job, you may or may not already routinely analyze sales numbers and the like. For example, if you're in sales, weekly, monthly, and quarterly sales reports are already very familiar reading matter for you. But, as a customer service rep, maybe you've never considered these reports to be your business. Make them your business now.

- **Look at the performance of the company's stock.** If you work for a publicly traded firm, track the performance of its stock for the preceding three to six months.

About Your Industry and the Marketplace

Just as you don't operate in a vacuum, your firm is hardly the only game in town. It has competitors, it is part of an industry, and it lives, breathes, thrives, sickens, or dies in a marketplace. Don't confine your research to material relating exclusively to your firm. Learn everything you can about your industry and current marketplace conditions as well as trends.

- Do a web search on keywords relating to your industry. Follow up all leads.

- Scan online and in-print publications for articles that inform you about industry trends and developments and that identify growth and opportunity areas as well as problems and pitfalls.

- Do web searches on the name of your boss, his boss, and other members of management with whom you may be familiar. Look for news about promotions, executive moves, and retirements.

- Look at product and service ads. These may tip you off to companies— yours and others—that are producing hot new merchandise and trend-setting services, or that are *failing* to create these items.

- Using the web or industry publications, analyze sales figures and trends. Is the marketplace in which your firm trades growing, contracting, or stable?

Remember to look for current or potential problems as well as opportunities. Also bear in mind that what may be a problem for your industry, and therefore your firm, can be an opportunity for you. Will new government regulations make brand-new demands on the industry? Maybe you can offer the willingness and expertise to help your firm comply with the new regulations. Doing so would make you a valuable commodity. Maybe even indispensable.

Check the Employment Landscape

Okay. Nobody's told you straight up that you'd better start looking for a job. But the fact is that you should *always* be looking for a job. If you haven't been doing this all along, starting now will accomplish three things:

1. It will help you build a lifeboat *before* your ship sinks. Trying to nail one together as the water laps around your neck is not easy.

2. It may find you a better job than you have right now—even if your current job is reasonably secure.

3. It may help you to assess the state of the employment market in your industry. Is there a lot of opportunity? Or is there a drought? Where are the opportunities? If you are in sales, and all the vacant jobs are in customer service, maybe it's time to expand your professional portfolio.

Read the want ads in industry-specific and professional publications and on similar websites. Now is also a good time to join a professional group or organization in your field. Doing so is a great way to network. Not only will you become acquainted with the state of opportunity in your industry, you are likely to meet potential alternate employers and get access to newsletters and magazines that publish industry-specific want ads. Make sure you check out the following networking websites:

- **LinkedIn (www.linkedin.com).** This is the biggest networking website for businesspeople in practically every field.

- **Plaxo (www.plaxo.com).** This site, which combines the functionality of an address book with the outreach of a social network, is finding increasing numbers of business users.

- **Tribe (www.tribe.net).** This networking site takes in the world of business, but also goes beyond, reaching into many aspects of everyday life.

- **Monster Networking (www.monster.com).** The nation's most popular job-search site, Monster offers a sophisticated networking area as well.

Poke around on the web, and you'll soon find that the problem is not too few sources of information, but almost too many.

About You

When you go to your boss to ask her how you're doing, you've got to go in packing heat. Go in with data on your company and department as well as on your industry and the relevant marketplace. But even after you have all this, you still need one more set of data. You need to know all about yourself.

This, you will find, is a much bigger, richer subject than your company or even your entire industry. It is so big that we'll need the next three chapters to cover it. Hold off on talking to your boss until you read them all.

CHAPTER 2

GET HOLD OF YOURSELF

"The unexamined life is not worth living," the Greek philosopher Socrates said, but how do you examine your life when you've got a job to do, a job to hold on to, a career to grow, and a family to care for? Where's the time? Who'll pay for it? And how can you do it without just driving yourself crazy?

These are all very good reasons to avoid intense introspection, but they miss the point. Learning about yourself is not something to do when you're not doing "your job." It's something that will enable you to do your job better. It is something that will enable you to get a better job. As a matter of fact, learning about who you are and what you have to offer should be at the very heart of everything you do. Fortunately, there is a way to focus your self-inquiry and target it, laserlike, so that it hits your working self spot-on. Turns out, it's all about knowing how to speak the right language.

Speak the Language of Business

People who become truly fluent in a second language do so by acquiring the habit of not merely speaking in the language, but thinking in it. To make yourself heard in the world of business, speak the language of business. To become fluent in that language, start thinking in it.

Begin by thinking about *yourself* in the language of business. It is a universal language. It doesn't matter where your particular employer's business is located or what the particular business makes, does, or offers. Every business speaks in a single language. It is the language of money. This means that when you think about yourself, when you take that mental inventory of your achievements and skills, do so in terms of money: the money you've made for your employer, the money you've saved your employer, and the money your achievements and skills will make and save for your employer in the days, months, and years to come.

Write Your Thoughts

Thinking is hard for all of us. Writing is hard for many of us. But just about anyone can think up then write down a list. Before you talk to your boss about your job, think (in the language of business, of course) about yourself. Keep a pen in hand or your fingers poised over the keyboard. Write as you think, creating a running list of what you've done for the company. Don't worry about organizing it. Don't try to censor or edit it. Just write it all down, one thing after another, as it comes and however it comes. Here's what a few items might look like:

Made 15 sales calls last week to established customers
Followed up on 23 leads for new customers
Made more than 50 cold calls
Filed my September expense report
Attended XYZ Conference

So far, the list says neither more nor less than that you're doing your job. Doesn't seem to be anything special here. However, start thinking in the language of business, and you may find yourself transforming the list into something more like this:

Made 15 sales calls last week to established customers, *who represent $XXX in business for the company during fiscal year 20XX*

Followed up on 23 new customer leads; *3 of these requested quotes on our widgets, representing potential sales of $XXX*

Made more than 50 cold calls with *the goal of growing this quarter's sales by X percent*

Filed my September expense report; *note that, while increasing customer site visits by X percent, I reduced my expenses by $XXX*

Attended XYZ Conference *and am preparing a report on a new XYZ process, which may save our department $XXX quarterly*

Inventory Achievement, Not Stuff

"What have you done for me lately?" is the question every employer asks every employee—mentally, if not out loud. Making a list like the first one is a good start, but if you really want to present your boss with a persuasive inventory of your value, this second list is far more convincing. In *all* communication, nouns and verbs are more powerful, more compelling, than adjectives and adverbs. That is because nouns and verbs are closer to reality, to the *actuality* you are trying to convey in *words*. In *business* communication, nouns and verbs are still better than adjectives and adverbs, but nouns and verbs linked to numbers—money made, saved, invested, spent—are best of all.

When you inventory "what you've done for your employer lately," focus on achievements rather than mere stuff. Always express those achievements in the language of business. Take care to translate your list out of the passive language of mere experience—how you passed the time during the last few days, weeks, quarters, or even years—into the dynamic terms of quantifiable achievement. Use your list of achievements to reveal more than the functions you have performed. Elevate the list to an inventory of achievement expressed in quantifiable value: "My report on the new XYZ process, which I completed the day before yesterday, shows how we can save $XXX every quarter, while turning around orders 20 percent faster."

Translate Achievements into Transferable Skills

After reading Chapter 1, you've taken steps to discover as much as you can about the current status of your department, your company, your industry, and the marketplace. This research should produce one of four results:

1. It may make you anxious and quite concerned about your present and future prospects with the firm.

2. It may alert you to opportunities for expanding, focusing, or refocusing your role in the firm.

3. It may make you both anxious about your current role within the firm *and* eager to expand, focus, or refocus it.

4. It may persuade you that you are a perfect fit in your present position and should do nothing.

If the fourth result describes your reaction, give the situation a little more thought. It *is* possible that you have found your perfect career niche. If, after thinking about it, you are convinced that this is the case, then just concentrate on continuing to do the best work you can. If, however, you do not feel that you are working up to your fullest potential, perhaps one of the first three results better describes your feelings about your research. If it does, the next logical step for you to take is a conversation with your boss.

Before you talk, be sure that you've undertaken the self-inventory just described, jotting down as many action items and functions you can think of, then translating these into the language of business by doing your best to attach a dollar value to each item, elevating these items into positive achievements for which you can claim full credit.

Having done your research and your inventory, take the next step: translate your achievements into your transferable skills. This will more sharply define what you bring to the workplace table—not just at your current job, but potentially at *any* job.

Skills constitute a very broad category, including the know-how you possess to do a particular job. If, for example, your job is to sell the Model A Widget, it's a good thing to be able to tell your boss "I know how to sell the Model A Widget." That is, it's a good thing as long as selling the Model A Widget is all you and your boss ever want you to undertake. A skill specific to a specific job is a good fit, but also a dead end. The last thing you want your boss to do is think of your job as a socket into which any number of others could just as easily be plugged. When you ask your boss for a raise or a promotion, and he believes wholeheartedly that you "know how to sell the Model A Widget," he may also believe that any number of others can be trained for the same job at a lower price.

Transferable skills, in contrast to mere *skills*, are know-how you own and you carry with you (they are also called "portable skills") rather than knowledge permanently affixed to a certain job. "I know how to sell the Model A Widget" expresses nothing more than the skill to do one certain job for one certain company, but "I know how to sell" expresses a transferable skill, something *you* bring to any employer.

You can make a list of your job-specific skills by glancing at your most recent job description, but it is up to you and you alone to compile an inventory of your transferable skills. You need to know what these are because they are yours. You take them with you. They represent your value to your current employer in your current job as well as your value to any prospective employer in a variety of jobs. Your current boss needs to know what your transferable skills are because they represent your future to her and the firm. If you possess skills A, B, and C and your current position requires only skill A, she needs to know that you are promotable to a position calling also for B and C, which will make the fullest use of you as an element of human capital. Your boss also needs to know that you are intrinsically valuable as human capital and not just a plug, like any other, to be inserted into an empty socket. Finally, your boss needs to be aware, keenly aware, that because you are valuable human capital, competing employers will value you.

If it's good to be able to answer "What have you done for me lately?" in compelling terms, it is even better to present your transferable skills, which answer the question "What will you do for me next?" The past is done, the present by definition does not last long, but the future holds all the promise. And it is the future to which your transferable skills lay claim. Know what they are and be prepared to present them when you have that talk with your boss or, for that matter, with anyone who has the power to advance your career, including colleagues and customers.

The Offer of Mastery

The future is not just yours to take, but also yours to offer. That offer consists of the benefits (to your boss and to the enterprise) of your mastery. Having prepared yourself with an inventory of your past achievements, use them as supporting evidence to build a case for your mastery of the knowledge and skills that promise years of indispensable performance.

Do not define mastery in personal terms—"My sales record this past quarter has given me a deep sense of satisfaction"—but in terms of benefit to your boss. Express this in the language of business: "My sales last quarter were up by XX percent from the previous quarter, and I'm positioned to bring in XXX dollars more this quarter. I'm anticipating an increase of XX percent."

Keep It Specific

Nothing is more useless than a vague inventory. Be sure that you have at the top of your mind a short list of *your most significant and specific* achievements. How do you decide what is "most significant"? Just think of the achievements for which you want to be remembered. *My most significant accomplishment this quarter is . . .*

- streamlining the problem-reporting process.

- increasing up-selling by 4 percent.

- increasing sales by 25 units.

- reducing order fulfillment errors by 8 percent over the last 90 days.

- reducing turnaround times on report processing by an average of two hours.

Don't Offer a Negative Inventory

As you examine yourself, you may well encounter deficiencies in your experience and achievements. Perhaps you have compiled an admirable sales record, but have (by your own estimation or some more objective measure) fallen short in up-selling (persuading established customers to upgrade to higher-priced offerings). It is essential to your own self-knowledge that you recognize such deficiencies, and you should be prepared to address them— but only if you are asked to. Be honest in your conversation with your boss, but don't confuse honesty with confession. Do not volunteer your negative inventory.

Convert Negatives

Do not volunteer your negative inventory, but do not put it out of your own mind. Take inventory of your assets as well as your liabilities. Know where you are vulnerable to criticism and prepare yourself to respond constructively. The objective is not to make excuses, but actually to convert the negatives into positives, liabilities into assets.

> **Boss:** I appreciate what you've done for us. I really do. Turnaround times in your department have come down, I know, but they're still not where they should be.
>
> **You:** I understand, but I think you'll agree that the department is moving in the right direction. Once we've streamlined process XYZ, which I'm working on now, we will bring turnaround down to a point even better than what you've specified.

Don't evade or deny the criticism. Instead, highlight where you are going and how you are improving rather than underscoring the present deficiencies, let alone apologizing for them.

Don't Just Make a Sale,
Create a Customer

Many of us are so eager to please that we give in to the temptation to rush to our boss and promise him anything. Resist this temptation. Take a deep breath—and take a leaf from the Great Book of Sales. Consider what it is that separates a pretty good salesperson from a truly great one. A good salesperson makes a sale. A *great* salesperson creates a customer.

As you take your self-inventory and prepare to present it to your boss, keep the greater goal in mind. Your purpose is not to settle for a single sale—the desperation play to hang on to your job—but to ensure that your boss becomes your best customer, someone who wants to do business with you now and in the future.

Your time is valuable. Use it to prepare yourself not only for the upcoming talk with your boss but for every subsequent interchange with him. Prepare to present yourself as what *this* boss and *every* other employer wants and needs: a standout employee not only with skills specifically suited to the job at hand but also possessed of the clear capability and character to manage anything thrown her way now or a year from now or ten years from now.

Take the Long View

Your objective is to persuade your boss—and others in your organization who have the power to help you—into wanting a long-term relationship with you. Whether you decided to stick around as long as she wants you is up to you, but it is to your advantage to have the option. Those who make their living in sales know that their best prospect is not at the other end of a cold call, but is always a current satisfied customer. And that is precisely what you want your boss to be. To ensure that she takes the long view of you and what you have to offer, make sure that you take the long view of yourself.

As you compile your self-inventory, don't stop with a tally of skills specific to your current job. Instead, focus on you, on the skills you carry with you rather than those a given job happens to require. You may already believe that you've got a pretty good handle on what you're good at. If you're asked to describe yourself as a businessperson, perhaps the first sentence that leaps to your mind is "I am persuasive." You reply: "I am persuasive. I can talk people into just about anything. That's my greatest skill."

But it's not—because persuasiveness is a description of a *trait*, not a *skill*, transferable or otherwise.

If you try to be more specific with something like "I am a persuasive salesperson," you're still not describing a transferable skill. This sentence is nothing more than a job description.

To take the long view of yourself, so that you can convince your boss to invest in you for the long term, you will have to figure out how to convert simple statements of traits and flat job descriptions into the exciting description of a transferable skill, an asset you own free and clear that makes you extraordinarily valuable to *any* employer anywhere and at any time. The next chapter will take you through the necessary conversion process, and it will show you how to dig down within yourself, right now, for the buried treasure you may not even know you possess.

CHAPTER 3

DIG FOR BURIED TREASURE

Ever walk into one of those cavernous "big box stores" at inventory time? A small army of workers, bar code scanners in hand, comb the shelves, counting everything—at least they count everything that is on display to customers. There is, of course, another part of the inventory that the casual shopper doesn't see. It's the search through the back room and the basement, ferreting out the stock that has yet to be displayed. Chapter 2 took you through the sales-floor inventory. It's time now to go to the back room and basement. Let's find out everything you've got, not just what's always on display. Let's dig for the buried treasure that marks you as indispensable.

"I Think I Am a Verb"

There's little chance that you will ever find a history book that mentions the names Ulysses Simpson Grant and R. Buckminster Fuller in the same sentence. The first was the hard-bitten, ultimately victorious general-in-chief of the Union army during the Civil War and the eighteenth president of the United States. The second was a maverick, hyper-innovative, multifaceted twentieth-century American engineer, architect, author, designer, inventor, and all-round futurist, creator of the geodesic dome, the Dymaxion house and car, as well as scores of other out-of-the box concepts. Grant died ten years before Fuller was even born. They never met. They never conversed. Yet they uttered, quite independently of each other, the same remarkable self-description: "I think I am a verb."

Fuller did not directly elaborate on this enigmatic sentence, but Grant did. He wrote it down shortly before he died from throat cancer in 1885; his remarkable note is quoted by William S. McFeely in his 1982 biography, *Grant*: "The fact is, I think I am a verb instead of a personal pronoun. A verb is anything that signifies *to be*; *to do*; or *to suffer*. I signify all three." Let's not worry about the suffering just now. It's the *being* and the *doing* that are key. What these two apparently unrelated figures had in common, men of different centuries and with vastly different careers, was the fact of their intense productive activity. They identified themselves not as static beings—neatly packed, wrapped, and tied packages of personality—but as doers: "beings" whose *being* consisted of *doing*. Even in thought, they were literally men of action. What they did—or, more accurately, what they were actively doing—defined them.

Learn from these two extraordinary men who were to all appearances worlds apart yet were united by the same conception of self. Be a verb.

Just Say It

"Just do it" is one of the best-known advertising slogans of our time. Your first step toward transforming yourself into a verb is actually a lot easier: *Just say it.*

Recall from Chapter 2 that it is common to mistake a *trait* for a description of a *transferable skill*. "I am persuasive" is a trait. Transform it by converting the adjective into a verb, so that "I am persuasive" becomes "I persuade." Now you have progressed from describing a trait to providing an active, dynamic description of what you actually do. You've gone a long way toward revealing yourself as a verb.

But don't stop here. Having transformed a trait into an active description of what you do, try transforming the kind of job description you might find in a résumé or employee handbook into a more vivid and personal description of a transferable skill. Like the description of what you do, this should also serve to reveal you as a verb.

Let's say you usually describe your job as "sales representative." Begin by understanding that all transferable skills fall into three categories. They relate to working with:

1. People

2. Data

3. Things

Next, make a decision. Decide whether "sales rep" chiefly involves working with people, data, or things. Although the job may involve all three categories—you may sell cars (things), which requires a knowledge of data (such as performance stats, prices, and so on)—the principal transferable skill a sales rep needs involves *people*; therefore, your description of a transferable skill becomes "I persuade people."

Ascend

Now you're really digging. By the simple magic of converting yourself into a verb, you have identified an important transferable skill that makes you (in the eyes of an employer) a valuable item of human capital.

Notice that "I persuade people" describes a function—that is, *doing something* with *people*, *data*, or *things*. Notice as well that, expressed as a function, "I persuade people" is a very powerful skill that is of tremendous value in a great many jobs. It can be made even more powerful, emerging as an asset that your boss (or, for that matter, any employer) will find highly compelling. Think of transferable skills as rungs on a ladder that ascends to levels of increasing complexity and, therefore, increasing value to an employer. *Persuading* is about at the middle of the ladder because it is a more complex people skill than merely *communicating*, which, in turn, is more complex than, say, *following directions*, which is a skill at the bottom of the ladder. On the other hand, *persuading* is less complex than *negotiating*, which is several rungs up, whereas *mentoring* is higher than *negotiating*.

What does this hierarchy mean to you?

The higher up on the ladder you are perceived to be, the more valuable you will appear to be. Convince your boss that you *persuade* people, and you may well keep your job in sales. Convince him that you *negotiate* with people, and you may open the door to a position as an account executive—or, at least, be perceived as a human capital asset with potential for growth beyond the sales rep level. If you can go beyond this, ascend the ladder even higher, demonstrating to your boss that you are proficient at *mentoring*, perhaps you will make yourself look like a potential vice president of sales.

The Deeper You Dig, the Higher You Go

The point of digging from one level to the next—in our example, from persuading, to negotiating, to mentoring—is to climb higher by digging deeper, not stopping until you reach your highest-level transferable skills. There are four reasons for putting in all this labor:

1. The higher the set of transferable skills you possess, the more distinctive and therefore valuable you are as an employee. Your objective is

to get as far away as possible from the plug-and-socket mentality. You want your job to look like something more than a generic socket and yourself like something more than a generic plug that happens to fit that socket. You want to make your job look demanding and full of potential and yourself look as if you'd be awfully hard, maybe even impossible, to replace.

2. Positions that require higher levels of transferable skills almost always pay more, have greater longevity, and promise more advancement than positions calling for lower levels of transferable skills.

3. Jobs that demand the higher levels of transferable skills are typically more than jobs; they're careers—which may be defined as jobs with a future.

4. The loftier your set of transferable skills, the more authority and control you will probably have on the job. At lower skill levels, employees are expected to follow directions; at higher skill levels, they are expected to practice creativity.

So, Dig In!

You can dig for your buried treasure without getting your hands dirty. Just start with three clean sheets of paper. At the top of one sheet, write "PEOPLE." On the second, write "DATA." On the third, put the word "THINGS." Below each of these headings, on each sheet, write "I am good at . . ." Next, complete the unfinished sentence in as many ways as you can think of for each category of transferable skills: people, data, and things. Here's an example:

People

I am good at . . .

 persuading

 selling

 helping customers decide what to buy

 explaining mechanical and technical things

 patient listening

Data

I am good at . . .

 finding

 reporting

 compiling

 interpreting

 analyzing

 combining

 drawing conclusions from

Things

I am good at . . .

 sorting

 arranging

 choosing

 assembling

 creating

 fixing

 understanding

 improving

If you're digging diligently, you should be able to list at least twenty-five items for each of the three headings. Try to list even more. Don't worry about editing or censoring your responses just now. Jot down all your ideas as they come. You'll have plenty of time to think about them later.

To Help You Dig

If you aren't satisfied with the progress you're making on blank sheets of paper, don't stop digging. Just get some help. Here are some forms to help you take a full transferable skills inventory. The first one is for People, the next for Data, and the third for Things.

TRANSFERABLE PEOPLE SKILLS INVENTORY

The transferable skills listed below are arranged in their approximate order of complexity, from lowest to highest; that is, "following instructions" is the first item listed and is a simpler skill than "coaching and mentoring," which is the last item. For each, rate your skill levels from 1 to 4, with 4 being the strongest. Be honest with yourself. Try to base your ratings on reality rather than on how you'd *like* reality to be.

With people as individuals, I am good at:

Following instructions	1	2	3	4
Serving	1	2	3	4
Listening	1	2	3	4
Communicating verbally	1	2	3	4
Communicating in writing (letters, memos)	1	2	3	4
Diagnosing, evaluating, and analyzing	1	2	3	4
Persuading	1	2	3	4
Recruiting and motivating	1	2	3	4

Selling	1	2	3	4
Instructing and training	1	2	3	4
Coaching and mentoring	1	2	3	4

With people in groups, I am good at:

Communicating	1	2	3	4
Representing	1	2	3	4
Guiding group discussion	1	2	3	4
Persuading and motivating	1	2	3	4
Formal public speaking	1	2	3	4
Performing and entertaining	1	2	3	4
Managing and supervising	1	2	3	4
Consulting and advising	1	2	3	4
Negotiating and resolving conflict	1	2	3	4
Leading innovation	1	2	3	4

TRANSFERABLE DATA SKILLS INVENTORY

Here is a similar guided inventory for your transferable skills in working with data. As with the people-skills inventory, the transferable skills listed go from least complex (lowest level) to most complex (highest level). The transferable skills listed here have also been broken down into groups and subgroups, which will help you analyze your skill set more accurately and completely.

With data, I am good at:

SORTING

Copying	1	2	3	4
Data entry	1	2	3	4
Record keeping and filing	1	2	3	4
Retrieving information efficiently	1	2	3	4
Helping others retrieve information	1	2	3	4
Memorizing and paying attention to detail	1	2	3	4

GATHERING

Compiling	1	2	3	4
Searching and researching	1	2	3	4
Observing (in order to gather data)	1	2	3	4

MANAGING

Comparing	1	2	3	4
Computing	1	2	3	4
Analyzing	1	2	3	4
Organizing, systematizing, prioritizing	1	2	3	4
Goal-oriented planning	1	2	3	4
Visualizing (drawing, creating graphics, etc.)	1	2	3	4
Synthesizing, developing, refining	1	2	3	4
Problem solving	1	2	3	4
Developing the "big picture" (vision)	1	2	3	4

CREATING

Daydreaming	1	2	3	4
Imagining	1	2	3	4
Improving (refining)	1	2	3	4
Designing	1	2	3	4
Inventing and innovating	1	2	3	4

TRANSFERABLE THINGS SKILLS INVENTORY

Rate your transferable skills in the area of "Things" just as you did with People and with Data; however, notice that the order of the larger groupings (*Working with Machinery and Vehicles, Working with Materials,* etc.) are not hierarchical with regard to one another. "Working with Machinery and Vehicles," for instance, does not represent a lower transferable skill set than that required for "Working with Materials." Within each grouping, however, the actual skills *are* arranged hierarchically, beginning with the lowest level and ending with the top level. Rate the items that are relevant to your job.

With things, I am good at . . .

WORKING WITH MACHINERY AND VEHICLES

Operating	1	2	3	4
Controlling (for example, driving)	1	2	3	4
Maintaining	1	2	3	4
Repairing	1	2	3	4
Assembling	1	2	3	4

WORKING WITH MATERIALS

Sewing, weaving, basic woodworking, etc.	1	2	3	4
Finishing	1	2	3	4
Carving	1	2	3	4
Sculpting	1	2	3	4
Precision handwork	1	2	3	4

CONSTRUCTION WORK

Rough carpentry, framing, etc.	1	2	3	4
Finish carpentry	1	2	3	4
Remodeling	1	2	3	4

WORKING WITH LIVING THINGS

Gardening	1	2	3	4
Farming	1	2	3	4
Caring for animals	1	2	3	4
Training and handling animals	1	2	3	4

BODY SKILLS

Strength	1	2	3	4
Endurance	1	2	3	4
Dexterity	1	2	3	4
Athletics	1	2	3	4

Examine Your Treasure

Using the blank-sheet method, the inventory rating method, or some combination of the two, draw up a list of eight to ten of your highest-level transferable skills.

For the blank-sheet method, review your lists and cross out those that are either your weakest skills or skills that seem to you at a low level. Pare the list down to just eight to ten of the highest-level transferable skills in which you feel strong. If you use the inventory rating method, focus on those higher-level skills you rate at 3 or 4. If you still end up with more than ten, eliminate all the 3s and retain only the 4s. If, after doing this, you *still* have more than ten, give the list some thought and edit out those skills that are at the lower levels.

Once you have winnowed your list down to eight to ten items, put each in a complete sentence that begins with "I am good at." Let's say that you've concluded that *negotiating* is one of your top skills. Write "I am good at negotiating."

This is just the beginning. Affix an object to the end of your sentence—for example: "I am good at negotiating *deals.*"

Take the next syntactical step by adding a word or a clause that highlights and explains the benefits of the object of your sentence. Like this: "I am good at negotiating deals *that please the buyer as well as the seller.*"

Perform this process of elaboration, refinement, and self-discovery for each of the eight to ten top-level transferable skills you have identified. By the time you are finished, you should have a rich, eloquent, yet concise profile of your key transferable skills. This will help you to present your value more effectively by setting yourself apart from the pack.

It's About Time to Start Playing Offense

So far, we've been concentrating on playing defense—proactively gathering knowledge to defend against the possibility of being laid off or let go. This is certainly important, and, depending on your circumstances and those of your employer, this may even be crucial. Nevertheless, playing defense is never sufficient. Defensive play is not enough to win. Even in the hardest of times, your goal should not be merely to hang on, but to continue building your career by acquiring more responsibility and authority, along with the rewards that go with these.

At the moment, it may look to you as if the best you can hope for is to keep from slipping and falling. In fact, you can—quite realistically—hope for much more. You can hope to climb.

Your Boss Is Your Best Prospect

I've said it earlier, but it bears repeating. Any successful sales professional knows that his best prospect for future sales is not some stranger at the other end of a cold call, but a current *satisfied* customer. That said, your likeliest prospect for career advancement is quite probably your current boss. This is assuming that you have created in her a satisfied customer. Nothing makes a better advertisement than a history of positive experiences.

In old-fashioned Hollywood movies about young executives on the rise, there is inevitably a moment when the boss throws an arm around the hero's shoulder and proclaims, "My boy, you're getting a promotion *and* a raise!"

Maybe it really used to happen that way—back in the day. But probably it never did, any more than it happens this way nowadays. People don't rise in an organization. They climb. And before they can climb, they need to find the ladder. Well, why go outside looking for a ladder when you've got one right in your own shop? Now that you know it's there, however, it's still up to you to start climbing.

Eyes Open

Fortunately, just as savvy employees understand that their current boss is probably their best prospect for achieving advancement, it is likely that your boss would rather develop the proven human capital he already has than take a chance on some unknown quantity from an outside company. This is why so many companies have a formal apparatus for announcing new positions internally and why many offer programs specifically geared to employee development.

The first move in playing offense is to know how, where, and when new positions are posted in your department or company. Usually, you'll find these on an internal website or in the employee section of the publicly accessible corporate site. Whatever the means and the forum, monitor the postings continually. If you see anything of interest, jump on it. Do it now. Others will. Others are.

To climb your company's corporate ladder, you'd better also start scaling the office grapevine. Often, word of an opportunity starts out as watercooler or break-room chat well before it's posted officially.

Be on the lookout for opportunities anywhere within your company—in your department, of course, but elsewhere as well. If you get hold of a lead that grabs your attention, ask questions. Pursue the lead aggressively. If, say, you hear that your boss is looking for a new right hand, talk to her. Tell her outright what you've heard and that you want the job. She will applaud your initiative, even if she denies the rumor.

The grapevine works two ways. You can pluck rumors from it, and you can plant information on it. Be proactive rather than passive. Put the word out: You are interested in advancement. You should be as specific as you reasonably can be: "It's about time for me to step into a supervisor position."

Don't Let a Ladder Become a Fence

If you've ever climbed any distance up a ladder, you know that it's strictly one step at a time, eyes on each rung as you go up. This is where the whole ladder metaphor stops being useful for anyone who believes the best defense in today's precarious job market is a bold offense. Instead of advancing step by step, one rung then the next, look up, *way* up. Imagine bigger. Let your ambitions be known, and if you learn of a position several rungs above you, try to pull yourself up to it, even though that means skipping the intervening rungs. You may not make it, but you will have made a point about your ambition and your commitment to the organization.

When Are Wild Dreams Too Wild?

The most successful people in any field, the real standouts, typically have one thing in common. They have all nursed wild dreams, and they have all acted on them.

But can a dream be *too* wild? Too unrealistic?

Not if you tame it just a bit.

You are a customer service rep. Your wild dream is to become vice president of sales. Is it likely that you can make the transition from the one to the other in a single bold leap? Realistically, no. But tame that wild dream by carving out a specialty for yourself, an area of expertise in which you excel, while simultaneously using this niche as a platform on which to exhibit not just your specialized, job-specific skills, but your transferable skills, and you will draw closer to that more distant rung.

Your goal is not to demonstrate what a great customer service rep you are, but, in the context of customer service, to demonstrate what a supremely competent and innovative person you are.

Make no mistake, your boss wants a great customer service rep. But he understands that this means finding a person who can do more than just read an employee manual. It requires a talented problem solver: someone who possesses the transferable skills required to solve problems.

If you stop thinking of yourself as a customer service rep and start thinking of yourself as a problem solver, you will present yourself—and others will begin to see you—in this way. Consider the following:

He: I can't figure out how to format this document. Are you any good with this software?

You: I don't specialize in that program, but, tell you what, I've always been a problem solver. Let me take a look for you.

Keep responding in this way. Keep translating requests for specific knowledge into occasions for delivering bravura demonstrations of your broader transferable skills, the skills that are your private property. In this way, you won't be identified as the go-to guy for solving XYZ software problems, but the go-to guy for solving problems, period. And, in any organization, problem solvers are indispensable.

Connect Yourself to Power

After you've mined your hidden treasure by identifying yourself with highly valued transferable skills, it is time to connect with people who have the power to promote you, to help you advance. If you are at a relatively early stage in your career, cast about for a mentor. All prospects should meet the following criteria:

1. The mentor should be a person to whom you have regular access.

2. He or she should be active in an area that not only interests you, but is appropriate to your background, skills, and training.

3. The mentor should be willing to mentor you.

4. The mentor should have the power to promote you.

After identifying a prospective mentor, approach her for business-related advice. Mild flattery is appropriate here. "Ms. Smith, you're the authority on XYZ in this office. How would you increase . . . ?" Make a habit of asking your prospective mentor questions. If she is responsive, chances are you have identified a good candidate.

Since cultivating a mentor requires an investment of your time as well as that of the mentor, don't waste your time on the powerless but instead focus on people who have the power to promote you and to do so sooner rather than later. For instance, if you are looking to enter management training in the Research Division, identify and talk to a senior manager in that division.

And don't forget your own boss. Depending on who he is and what he's like and how the two of you feel about each other, he may be the very last person you want as your mentor; on the other hand, just as your current firm may offer the most promising prospects for career growth, so your current boss may stand out as your most obvious mentoring candidate.

Approach your prospective mentor by asking for nothing and instead making an offer or two:

1. "I've been selling widgets for two years, and it has taught me a lot about what our customers value most. I'd like to begin applying what I've learned to managing accounts in your department."

2. "I want to take what I've learned to you."

3. "I could solve a few problems for you."

Over a period of months you can develop the mentoring relationship into an opportunity for promotion. Again, ask for nothing. Offer value instead:

1. Say nothing about what you need.

2. Propose all that you can offer your department and the company, provided that you are assigned increased responsibility.

3. Propose all that you can do for the boss. Paint a self-portrait of a problem solver. Show how you can make this person's life easier and more successful.

4. Build your case. Do not expect your boss to have committed your résumé to memory. Present a list of solid achievements.

5. Build a self-promotional vocabulary that is short on adjectives but long on verbs and numbers: actions and results. Speak the language of business, the language of dollars made and dollars saved.

Here is an example of offering value to gain a promotion:

Working with you has taught me a great deal about the relationship between sales and customer service. I'd like to put what I've learned to work for us. My experience working with you has convinced me that service reps could and should be working more effectively with sales reps to increase sales, especially up-selling. Right now, there is a gap between sales and service. I want to work on closing that gap, making the connection between the sales and service functions seamless. You know that in the six months I've been working with you, sales have increased by an average of 12 percent. Most of this increase has been in the area of up-selling and accessories sales. And much of this increase has come from work I've done with the service reps, encouraging them to promote merchandise themselves rather than send customers back to sales. So far, this work has been casual—something I've done in addition to my other duties. I would like to propose a new position—service sales manager— and I would like to design it and, of course, fill it. I can promise even better numbers than I've delivered so far.

A lot of people find it hard to speak up for themselves, even when business is booming. In tough times, seeking to rise may seem pushy or at least unrealistic. But the truth is that a tough time is the very best time to put your optimism, faith in the firm, and eagerness to serve on display. Bold, eager, and able people are always valuable. In times that cry out for maximum effort, they are indispensable.

CHAPTER 4

TAKING AIM

The first two chapters were about assessing your current job situation, getting in position to hold on to what you have, and not only holding on to it, but even rising within it. The chapter you've just finished reading was about moving from a more or less defensive strategy to a more assertive attack mode.

Now it's time to take the positive approach a big step ahead. Look for open doors—potential as yet unharvested, opportunities that no one else has grabbed, important jobs that need doing—and walk through. And if you feel one of those doors beginning to close on your future, don't waste too much time trying to shoulder it open. It hurts, and you can't keep your shoulder against that door forever, can you? Consider letting it close—as long as you're ready to go open another. This chapter will show you how to find other doors without leaving your present employer. You will find strategies for assessing where you're at in your current job and for opening up new possibilities within it, which will benefit you and your employer—which is, of course, another benefit for you.

Set New Goals

First find that other door. Time to set new goals. We're not talking about a Plan B—some kind of stopgap, like taking a salary cut or accepting a demotion (though, as a matter of immediate survival in some cases, you may have to do something of the kind, at least temporarily)—and we're not talking about simply turning your back on your current employer (that is the subject of Chapter 12). Instead, this chapter is about applying everything you've learned in the first three chapters to remodel yourself in the eyes of your present employer. The idea is not to hold on to what you've got, but to make what you've got even better so that you can grow with it. By setting new goals, you can reposition yourself within the company and present yourself to your employer in a new way, yet without asking her to roll the dice on an unknown quantity.

What does your boss want? The impossible: Something entirely new that's worked well in the past. Give it to her.

Redefine yourself in terms of new goals, and you have a fair chance of delivering to your current employer precisely this impossible commodity. You are a known quantity, a proven human asset. You've worked well in the past. Challenging times are the very time to present your old self as something entirely new.

Tell Some Familiar Stories in a New Way

The digging you did in the last chapter may have yielded enough "treasure" to help you see yourself in new ways and, equally important, to allow you to show yourself to your current boss in those new ways. But now that your back is sore from all that shovel work, don't be downhearted if it didn't produce enough "A material" to impress your boss in the way you want to impress him. The fact is that, strangely enough, few people do what you're in the midst of doing right now. Very few of us actually stop to *think* about our jobs, let alone our careers. Depending on the industry you're in, the part of the world you happen to occupy, the particular time at which you entered the labor market, and the luck of the draw, you might get through a career without ever having to think much about what you're doing. Besides, it can be hard work to figure out just what your job *could* or *should* be. If simply taking inventory has not given you everything you need, then it's time to tell yourself some old stories in new ways.

Some Homework

Here's the assignment. Call to mind a single successful action or achievement for which you were responsible. It is best if the episode is directly related to your job, but it does not absolutely have to be. Start writing about it. In contrast to the list-making projects in the previous chapter, don't approach this as a free-form exercise. Instead, adhere closely to the following plotline:

1. State your goal, what you set out to do or accomplish by the action you are writing about.

2. Just about every good story revolves around a problem or a conflict. You need to write a story that has at least one of these. So, after stating your goal, describe at least one problem, conflict, or obstacle blocking the path toward your goal.

3. Next, narrate what you did to solve the problem(s), resolve the conflict(s), or overcome the obstacle(s). Narrate this process in detail step by step.

4. Don't leave your reader hanging. Come to a definite conclusion by fully describing the outcome, including the effect and significance of the outcome. In other words, explain just what it was that you accomplished.

5. Finally, if you have not already incorporated this into #4, provide an objective evaluation of your achievement. To the degree that it is possible to do so, quantify the outcome in the language of business: dollars saved, dollars made.

While you should follow this outline, don't worry about producing a piece of literature worthy of a Pulitzer Prize. It's not necessary to come up with the story of how you single-handedly saved your company (unless you really have done so). Any solid achievement that produced tangible value for the company, for others, or for yourself will do very nicely. Consider the following example from a customer services representative.

This is a story about how I delivered exceptional service to a client who was in urgent need of my help.

Two months ago, ABC Widgets phoned me. They were in a total panic. Their problem was that they could not bypass a software roadblock. Somehow, they had improperly set the password coding, and now they could not execute any transactions for their customers. That was the reason for the panic, and it was a pretty good reason.

I understood how they felt, but I also knew that I couldn't let *their* panic infect me and compromise my judgment. My training had taught me that the first and most important priority was to protect ABC's security as well as ours. A software roadblock isn't always easy to overcome, especially over the phone, because of the possibility of a security breach. So I knew I had to move carefully, no matter how frantic the client got, and take the time required to maintain the security protocol that benefits both the client and us. But I also knew that I had to do this without making the client more frantic than they already were—and without suffering an emotional backlash from them, which could even cost us the account.

So, after assuring the people on the other end of the line that we would resolve the problem together and that I would stay on the case until it was fully resolved, I took out the security manual checklist and proceeded to follow all the rules and to get all necessary confirmations from ABC to insure that I was dealing directly and only with authorized people before I dug into the password problem.

At first some of them were pretty defensive and even irritable. Clearly, they just wanted to get into the problem. I understood: They needed an immediate solution. However, I remained professional and explained why it was in their interest that I follow the security protocol to the letter.

I began by apologizing for needing to check for a security breach. Then I explained why I needed to do this, and I reviewed the value ABC received by my following the rules. I also assured them I didn't think any of them were hackers, and I even complimented them on the efficiency of their own internal security, pointing out that, combined with our systems, it made for a very tough security shield that gave the company's customers a real value and was therefore a selling advantage for them. In other words, I explained that by adhering to the protocol, time-consuming as it was, we were protecting ABC's reputation in the marketplace.

By following the protocol, I was able to get around the roadblock and get ABC Widgets up and running again—while also preserving full security for them and for us.

I'm proud of what I did. In a stressful situation like that one, when time was critical and the customer really did need immediate action, I was able to maintain focus and keep us both going in the right direction. I did feel pressured to bypass the security protocol—and I had the online tools on my end to do just that. However, I resisted the temptation because I knew the value of the protocol, and I was able to communicate its strategic value to the client. In the end, ABC's general manager called to thank me personally. And that felt really good.

What I took away from the experience were four important lessons:

Number 1: When you have to confront a frustrated customer, it is key to express empathy and even to apologize for the current circumstance. Saying something like "I'm sorry this has happened" is not the same as accepting responsibility for a problem you didn't cause, but it still goes a long way toward lowering the other person's frustration level.

Number 2: Nothing is more aggravating to a customer than saying you're following the rules or company policy or just doing what you're told to do. Follow the rules, but also take the time to explain the value those rules represent, the value you are offering your client. If I had met more resistance from the people at ABC, I would have taken time to explain the kind of disasters that could occur if ABC's computers had somehow been breached and we were being duped and exploited into helping hackers break into their system.

Number 3: It is important to be firm, but also to assure the customer that you are not accusing anyone of wrongdoing.

Number 4: Try to turn a negative situation into a positive one. I took the time to point out that the security protocol we were following was actually a big value added for ABC customers and that it gave ABC a good selling point and competitive edge.

Evaluating Your Homework

Try to write at least three or more stories like this one, each starting with a goal, introducing a problem, explaining your solution, stating the outcome, then evaluating the outcome. Read them over. Think about them. Compare each story with the checklist of people, things, and data transferable skills you created in Chapter 3. Decide which transferable skills these stories demonstrate. Doing all this should:

1. Enable you to define and describe your transferable skills.

2. Enable you to discover transferable skills you didn't even know you had.

3. Enable you to identify job and career goals.

As you can see from the list above, this homework assignment is, first and foremost, for you. It will help you to learn more about your strengths so that you can define or redefine job and career goals. But the results are not exclusively about *self*-discovery. Telling stories and thinking about them will also enable you to bring concrete examples of achievement to your conversations with your boss. Make a list of these examples and review it—and add to it—repeatedly. When you ask your boss for a job that offers greater responsibility, more rewards, and a bigger stake in the future, she will likely respond with a number of questions of her own. Whatever she actually asks, you can be sure that there is one question uppermost in her mind: *What have you done for me lately?* Do your homework, and you'll be able to answer this fully, clearly, concretely, and—therefore—persuasively.

Are You Satisfied with Your Job?

The toughest of times, the times that make you worry about the future, are the times when the future is your strongest ally. The value of the future is not the *hope* that things will improve, but the very reason for your taking steps to actually improve things. What is more, the future does not belong exclusively to you; it also belongs to your boss and your company. If, in a difficult time, you can persuade your boss that you and he do have a future together, you will most likely accomplish a lot more than just hanging on to your job.

Any time, in any economy, is the right time to ask yourself: *Am I satis-*

fied with my job? But hard times? They are the *perfect* time to use your list of transferable skills as a yardstick to measure just how your current situation suits you or fails to suit you. When times are hard, you really have to know the full value you offer an employer. Measuring that value against your current job is a great way to assess it fully, honestly, and persuasively. Does your current work allow you to make use of what you're best at, make use of what sets you apart? Does it increase your value as human capital? Or is some of the best part of you going to waste each and every day at the job?

What? *More* Homework?

There is neither exact science nor mystical magic to evaluating your feelings about your current situation. Just do this: Take out a piece of paper and fold it lengthwise, so that you have two columns. Head the left one "I like" and the right "I don't like." Under the left-hand heading, list everything you like about your job; under the right-hand heading, everything you don't like. Do not be surprised if you find that a few things find their way into *both* columns. Most people have mixed feelings about any number of things.

Don't mistake this exercise for a rehash of what you did in Chapter 3. In fact, what's especially important about drawing up this list is that you will find yourself jotting down much more than your transferable skills. This new list will be filled with other items related to the workplace, including, for instance, the physical environment as well as the people you work with; the kinds of tools and other materials involved in the work; your salary; the demands the work makes on your time and the kinds of clients and customers you serve, in addition to the purpose of the job; the kinds of tasks it involves; the talents, knowledge, training, and skills it requires; the level of prestige it confers (or fails to confer); and more. Whatever else your current job gives you or fails to give you, it does provide an *experience*, and experience is always valuable for what it tells you about yourself, about what you like and don't like, and about what you need and do not need, what you want and do not want.

The Status Quo—Comfortably Fatal

Your self-analysis may tell you that you love your job. It may tell you that you hate your job. More likely, it will suggest that your feelings are somewhere in between these extremes. But don't worry, learning the truth about how you feel will *not* force you to walk out the door and onto the breadline.

- If you love your job and want desperately to hold on to it, everything you've learned or will learn in this book will help you to do that.

- If you hate your job and want to make a change, everything you've learned or will learn in this book will help you to do that.

- If (like most people) you are in between the extremes of total satisfaction and total dissatisfaction, everything you've learned or will learn in this book will help you develop the work you currently have into something that promises to be better for you, your boss, and your company.

How to Create Satisfaction

Satisfaction is not just about being happy with your job. It's also about satisfying others—that is, satisfying your "customers," whether these are actual clients (external customers) or your colleagues or boss (internal customers). You produce a product every day—your work, the value you offer the organization—and as with any other producer, your success depends on creating satisfied customers.

Creating customer satisfaction requires that you consistently meet or exceed the expectations of your customers. In other words, you have to do really good work—and there is no faking that. This said, you should *not* depend exclusively on the quality of your work to "speak for itself." Sure, we all know of companies that survive and even prosper exclusively by word of mouth based on the sterling reputation of their products. But for every firm that operates this way, there are untold numbers that at the very least supplement word of mouth by marketing and advertising. It is the rare company that neglects these and survives, let alone thrives.

So think about what you do. Regardless of your particular job, you are, first and foremost, a producer, which means that you must consistently produce excellence if you expect to grow in your career. But, like the overwhelming majority of other producers, you should do more.

You should also be a marketer.

Market Yourself

Marketing any product begins by identifying a market or markets for it. In other words, marketing begins by identifying your best potential customer. At this point, you already have a customer—your boss—so you have two choices. The first is to adjust your product offering and presentation to suit your customer. The second is to look for a different customer, a new boss, which means a new job. These two choices aren't necessarily mutually exclusive. You can seek to satisfy your current customer while also seeking a new one. The great thing about thinking about your job in terms of satisfying your customers is that if you can figure out how to satisfy one customer, you may well discover the secrets of satisfying many.

The first three chapters have offered guidance on how you can define, present, and explain the value you offer your boss or any other employer. The key point to bear in mind in this chapter, however, is that you should not consider this a passive process: "I offer X, Y, and Z. Take it or leave it." Instead, never stop thinking like a marketer, and always *position* yourself.

Positioning is the way in which a product, service, or an entire company is perceived by the best potential customer for that product, service, or company. Do for yourself what you would do for your company. Create a position, an image or a set of beliefs, for your marketplace. Any firm that invests in advertising strives to ensure that all of its advertising is based on positioning. You, who are endeavoring to advertise your set of transferable skills to your boss (and to others), should likewise take steps to position yourself.

Know that, whatever your product, whatever your merchandise, there are three dimensions to any market position:

1. **Benefit:** This is the emotional reason to "buy" your "product"; that is, the benefit is essentially how your product promises to make the customer feel.

2. **Target:** Your ideal customer or set of customers.

3. **Competition:** The others operating in your marketplace and vying for the same customers.

Of these three dimensions, there may be little you can do about the second and nothing you can do about the third. While it is true that you may decide to seek another boss—get another job—doing so, especially in tough times, involves a formidable set of risks, so let's assume that your most immediate priority is to remain with your current employer. If that is the case, your customer has already been chosen for you. It is your boss. As for the third dimension, the fact is that your competition is your competition. They are present, you did not hire them and so cannot fire them, and thus they are a given, a fact of your professional life.

This leaves the first dimension, *benefit*. This one is entirely yours to control.

To begin, we must be careful to distinguish *benefits* from *features*. Some years back, Federal Express constructed an advertising campaign around the slogan "Relax. You sent it FedEx." This was a prime example of advertising a benefit as opposed to a feature. The key *feature* of the FedEx product is reliable overnight delivery. The *benefit* promoted here, however, was peace of mind—a feeling.

Having identified your key transferable skills, you already know how to describe what you might call the features of your product. If you say, "I am good at negotiating prices that satisfy both the seller and the customer," you are describing—in some detail—one of the key features you offer employers. To position yourself more effectively in the job market, however, you must translate such features into benefits.

Ask yourself how the key features or set of features of the "product" you offer deliver benefits to your customer—your boss. Remember, a benefit is primarily emotional. It is about creating a certain desirable feeling or state of mind in your customer. The statement of a product *feature* "I am good at negotiating prices that satisfy both the seller and the customer" can be converted into a *benefit* by saying "I create satisfaction" or even "I will make your life easier, by ensuring satisfaction for us and for our customers."

Advertising agencies collect handsome fees for analyzing, defining, and selling the benefits of their clients' products. Doing this can be hard work that calls for the services of talented copywriters. Fortunately, your job is much easier. Whereas defining the benefits of a particular brand of deodorant requires understanding a wide range of buying patterns and emotional motives among a variety of consumers, your principal customer, your boss, like any employer, really has but a single motive. She wants to save and to make more money. You are therefore standing on solid ground if you can translate your set of transferable skills into factors that will benefit the bottom line, as in this example:

> I am good at negotiating prices that satisfy both the seller and the customer. What I'm saying is that I don't just make the sale, I make every sale a really good sale, a sale that creates satisfaction, which means repeat business over the long term. You can rely on me to add to the bottom line this quarter, as well as next quarter and, in fact, quarter after quarter.

Make It Real

Marketing can work wonders, but it can't work miracles. To credibly market excellent performance, you do have to perform at an excellent level and do so consistently. Before you take the next step, which is marketing yourself directly to your boss, review this prelaunch checklist. Do the following statements accurately describe you?

1. I *really* know my job in depth.

2. I know and do my job so well that it would be very hard to replace me in it.

3. I am open to change. I embrace new technology or improved procedures.

4. I look for better ways to do things, and I bring these into my work.

5. I volunteer more than the average worker.

6. I am a team player.

7. I look for extra work that benefits the company and interests me.

8. I consistently demonstrate my interest in what I do.

9. I offer constructive suggestions for improvement, innovation, and the like.

10. I am reliable.

11. I complete assigned projects on time.

12. I show up where and when I'm expected.

Be brutally honest in your answers. They aren't a judgment against you, but a diagnosis of the reality that must serve as a sturdy platform for your self-marketing effort. Examine any statement to which you cannot respond with a frank *yes*. Ask yourself what you must do to get to that *yes*. List those steps, and take those steps before you talk to your boss.

Build New Markets

Having done your homework and having determined that your platform of actual performance is rock solid, you are now ready to talk to your boss in a way that will sell him on the benefits you offer. Sometimes, doing this successfully requires thinking outside of the box that defines your current position. Even if your sole objective is to remain with your current employer, don't necessarily restrict your thinking to remaining in your current job just the way it is.

Savvy career builders always put the emphasis on building. Some opportunities are just waiting to be found. Let's say you are in customer service for Product Line A, and there is a better position in sales for that same product line. Think beyond customer service and talk your way into sales via the vast experience you already have with Product Line A. But don't even restrict yourself looking for existing opportunities. If the opportunity you need is not waiting to be found, create it yourself.

Even when you've made the decision to think outside of the box, remember the old saying, tired though it may be: *Build on what you have.* The most feasible route to the creation of a new position almost always runs straight through your current department, where you have firsthand experience and in which you have created credibility in the form of a quantifiable track record.

Of course, before you start building a new position for yourself, you should find a good reason for starting construction. Here are five:

1. You see a genuine, perhaps even pressing need for the position in your firm or department.

2. The positions currently available fail to satisfy your needs and aspirations.

3. The positions currently available do not allow you to make full use of your unique transferable skills.

4. The positions currently available do not constitute your dream job. (And why shouldn't you have a shot at your dream job?)

5. You want a position that is uniquely yours, one that you own. By creating your position, you own it. Ownership carries risks, and they may be substantial, but ownership also offers an opportunity for increased creativity within your organization. You can put your stamp on the position, and you can become a driving force within it. It is one thing to make yourself indispensable—a very good thing it is, too—but it is even better to create for yourself a job that is indispensable.

What You Need to Create Your Own Job

Creating your own job within your current organization is a real challenge, but it is one of the most exciting and fulfilling career moves you can make. It stakes a claim to a place in your firm, which is all the more important during troubled times.

The first step is to learn in depth how your department or organization works and how, in turn, it works with other departments. Imagine that you are an outside consultant hired by your department or organization to make recommendations for improvements. Proceed accordingly.

1. Consider how the department could be improved by the addition of such-and-such a position or the replacement of an existing position by a new one.

2. Work out your recommendations in detail.

3. After deciding what facts and figures you need to support your recommendations, start gathering this data.

4. Draw up scenarios demonstrating the benefits of the new position.

5. Combine these scenarios with your facts and figures and with data relating to your own performance in your current position, so that you can present yourself as the ideal candidate for the position.

Be aware that your company may simply be unable to move you into a new or redesigned position. Even if this is the case, you can still take these five steps to identify new opportunities for projects or for expanding your sphere of responsibility. Take note as well of the common saying that you must do the work for the position you want long before you actually get it. Take these steps to show your readiness for the desired position and to persuade your boss of just how valuable you are. At the very least, you'll be demonstrating that you care about the company's progress and that you actively seek to identify problems and find solutions for them. In other words, by following this advice, you will be marketing your work ethic and thus putting yourself at the head of the line for a new position when it becomes available. No positive effort is wasted.

Other Strategic Moves

We are naturally conditioned in business either to take the lead, follow, or get out of the way. A career is seen in one dimension and one dimension only: up. A move in any other direction seems an admission of something less than success, maybe even a confession of outright failure.

At any time, but especially in a challenging economy, you should open your mind to more than a single dimension of movement. *Up* is not the only strategically viable direction for a successful career. Sometimes a lateral move is called for, either as a means of short-term survival within the company—a way to stay employed with the firm—or as a trade-off, a move to a position at roughly the same level of compensation, but one that provides some other benefit, in the form of intellectual or emotional satisfaction or greater potential for future growth, for example. Your perception of the future may even drive you to make a downward move. There are times when, to keep from getting locked into a career track that will ultimately offer less money, longevity, security, or growth, you may choose to make a lateral or even a downward move that may position you for greater advancement later.

In some ways lateral moves are actually easier to make than moves up the salary ladder. Your boss can see that your action is not motivated solely by a salary increase—because there is none—but by a genuine desire for the position. This suggests a deep commitment to the organization and a passion for its mission.

In other ways, however, the lateral move presents a greater difficulty than the more conventional upward climb, especially if you decide to move laterally out of your current department. Your boss may find it easier to accept a move made for reasons of money versus one motivated by a desire for something intangible this boss apparently cannot offer. She may even think you don't like or respect her.

Consider alternatives to rising, but pursue them only when you have a strong *strategic* reason for making the lateral move. Always weigh future gains against current risks. This is even more important if you decide to make a downward move, but also be keenly aware that serial lateral moves can be career killers. If you seem to make a habit of moving from one same-salary position to another, you risk sending a message of unreliability. No one wants to invest time and energy in a subordinate who has a record of bugging out for no good reason.

Selling the New Job

Having created a set of scenarios and matched yourself to a proposed new position, new project, or expanded responsibilities, you now have to make your case to your boss.

The one thing to avoid is the appearance of presenting your idea as a fix-it for something your boss has wrecked. To avoid giving the impression that you are mopping up after your boss, steer clear of criticism and negativity. Instead, emphasize the positive contributions you intend to make: "I'd like to speak with you about how I can make a bigger, more valuable contribution to our department. I need your take on some ideas I've been working out."

Some people—even some very bright people—will have a knee-jerk negative response to anything that seems radically new. They just can't help it.

Nevertheless, you can minimize the reflexive objection to novelty by deliberately easing the transition from the status quo to the great unknown by presenting your proposal not as a *new* position at all, but as simply a logical, natural extension of your current responsibilities. For many managers, continuity is high priority. Satisfy them by honoring the high position in which they place it.

Present yourself as an asset to the department. Don't start off by proclaiming the need for a brand-new position or a new project. Instead, as you explain to your boss how you see your expanded role, let him point out that what you are talking about is redefining your present job, launching a new project, or even creating an entirely new position. It is always easier to sell someone on his own idea; therefore, let the concept of a new project, a redefined position, or a whole new job emanate from the boss, not you. Let him claim an ownership stake in the idea.

To lead your boss in the desired direction, use inclusive pronouns:

we
us
our

instead of the singular pronouns:

I
me
you

Also employ "what if" language":

Wouldn't it be great if . . . ?
What if we had X capability in-house . . . ?

If we had someone to do X, then we would be able to . . .

If we had someone to do X, then we wouldn't have this problem in the future.

This could be a great opportunity, if we . . .

Your objective is to create the verbal environment most likely to move your boss's thoughts in the direction *you* want them to go.

Another way to give your boss a proprietary stake in your idea is to connect what you want with what your boss has already indicated that he wants:

This reminds me of what you said back in February, about more closely coordinating Service with Sales so that we don't miss out on opportunities to sell accessories. I've been reaching out to Service, as you know, but we really need to develop a dedicated coordinator position to achieve the consistency of connection that we had talked about early in the year.

It can be difficult to relinquish your hold on an idea. It is natural to want to claim credit for what we originate. But your objective is to rise and to grow, not to get a pat on the back—good as that may feel. Sharing ownership of your initiative will substantially improve the chances of your dream becoming a reality of the enterprise. And, in the end, it is the reality you succeed in creating—not the proposal, not the idea, no matter how good—that finally matters to you and your career.

Standing Out and Fitting In

The indispensable employee fits into the organization even while standing out. How? Chapter 5 begins Part Two with a set of simple formulas for building the boundless value of rapport and integrating yourself into the workplace culture—without becoming invisible in the process. Chapter 6 transforms the knife-in-the-back image of "office politics" by discarding it in favor of "office diplomacy": the art of creating satisfaction among staff, colleagues, and bosses and, in the process, creating rapport and recruiting allies throughout the workplace. Chapter 7 moves you beyond diplomacy and rapport to branding, with a dozen tactics to brand you as indispensable. And because business is never really about business but all about people doing business, Chapter 8 provides a solid blueprint for building highly productive relations with the person you call your boss. Chapter 9 guides you in dealing effectively with the real hard cases in any organization. Get the best even from "difficult" people, and you will find that you have become truly indispensable.

CHAPTER 5

UNCOMMON COURTESY

You sleep a third of your life. Of the remaining two-thirds, at least half is spent among your coworkers, bosses, and subordinates. You don't just *work* with these people. You *live* with them, and you do so for about the same number of waking hours in any given week that you live with your family. Obviously, it is in your best interest to make a life with them that is productive, rewarding, and—well—livable. This is a prerequisite to becoming indispensable in the workplace.

The indispensable man or woman creates rapport with everyone in the workplace, which, these days, like any other community, is usually richly diverse in culture and background. It is up to you to see for yourself and to persuade others to recognize that the common goals of the enterprise outweigh all differences, conflicts, and private motives.

Korporate Karma

We're told to avoid speaking in clichés because they make us sound imitative, boring, and generally unthinking. These are all good reasons not to use them, but, even more to the point, as sure as Isaac Newton told us that every action produces an equal and opposite reaction, so every cliché pulls along another cliché that says exactly the opposite. Supposedly, it was baseball manager Leo Durocher who coined back in 1939 one of the most enduring clichés of all: "Nice guys finish last." Sounds convincing, but, true to form, there's another cliché to cancel this one out: "What goes around comes around."

Durocher was a successful baseball manager, no doubt about it, but the second cliché—and no one knows who said it first—has a bit more to back it up. For one thing, there's the Golden Rule: *Do unto others as you would have them do to you.* For another, there is the Hindu and Buddhist concept of karma, roughly the idea that what *you* do shapes *your* destiny. Do good and good will tend to be done to you. Do bad and . . . well, you get it: *What goes around comes around.*

The workplace is not a static environment into which you and others are simply plopped. Like any other community, it is dynamic, continually shaped, created, reshaped, and recreated by what you and others do and say. Follow the Durocher cliché, and you will tend to build a dog-eat-dog, knife-in-the-back gladiatorial arena to which you are forced to devote half your waking life. Follow the karmic model, however, and you will influence the creation and maintenance of a more nurturing and productive environment. Not only is it likely to be a far more pleasant place in which to invest your waking hours, it is also more likely to create the collaborative, communal success on which your personal well-being depends. If all the members value the community in which they have a stake, they will almost surely value *you* as a part of that community.

Always Walk a Step Beyond

If your idea of being a "nice guy" is rolling yourself in a ball of passivity and letting come what may, you can expect to be kicked around and, quite probably, sooner or later, kicked out. Creating good workplace karma does not mean "letting things slide" or "taking it on the chin." What it does require is the active exercise of walking a step beyond your own ego. It requires the vigorous application of empathy.

Recall the last time you bought something from a really good salesperson. People who have a positive talent for selling are like fine musicians. Their art is made up of a thousand unique nuances. Nevertheless, all successful salespeople do at least two things:

1. They take the focus off of themselves.

2. They put the focus on you, the customer.

"You've got to buy this car. I need the commission to pay this month's rent." That may well be what the salesperson is thinking on the showroom floor as he lifts the hood and invites you to have a look, but it is certainly not what he says to you. In fact, if he's any good at selling, he doesn't begin with a declaration of any kind. Instead, he asks *you* questions aimed at finding out how he can satisfy *you*.

The secret of selling—whether the product is an automobile or your own value as an employee—is first and foremost to discover the wants, needs, concerns, desires, anxieties, and aspirations of your "customer." Once these have been ascertained, your next step is to address them as fully as you can. The single word for this selling process is *empathy*, a thorough identification with another human being.

Your motive for empathy is not altruistic self-sacrifice, but the knowledge that in order to get you've got to give, and in order to give effectively you've got to know what the other person wants. Always bear in mind what distinguishes the good from the great salesperson. A good one makes sales. A great one makes customers. Just as you must see beyond your own ego to create empathy and rapport, so you have to think beyond each specific thing *you* want and focus instead on ensuring that each interaction with subordinates, colleagues, and bosses is satisfying to *them*.

Mutual Trust, Emotional Affinity

Every time you interact with your boss or a coworker you are presented with an opportunity to create or enhance rapport, which we may define as a relationship of mutual trust and emotional affinity.

A given interaction may be momentous in your eyes—asking for a promotion, for example—or it may be nothing more than saying a pleasant good morning as you pass in the hall. Rapport is built on interactions great and small. It is a cumulative product of these. By the same token, rapport can be eroded and torn down by interactions great and small. So, whatever you do and say, always think about building rapport instead of wrecking it.

While rapport is cumulative, often developing gradually over a period of years, it may also be accelerated by using a *helping vocabulary* every chance you get.

SPEAKING THE LANGUAGE OF RAPPORT
The three most basic components of a helping vocabulary are the forms of the first-person plural pronoun:

> we
>
> us
>
> our

Look for occasions to move the conversation from *I* and *you* to *we, us,* and *our*. For instance, your boss complains: "I can't seem to get Auditing to deliver their monthly reports on time." In choosing among the response options you have, make your selection with the objective of building and enhancing rapport.

> **Response 1:** "You've really got a problem." Could be worse. At the very least, this response indicates that you are listening. But that *you* pronoun serves to separate your boss (the *you*) from yourself (the *I*). Rapport is never about separating. It is always about joining.
>
> **Response 2:** "We've really got a problem." By joining the *you* and the *I*, the pronoun *we* builds rapport, making it a part of the very language you speak.

Now keep building. "We've really got a problem" is good, but it cries out for a follow-up.

> **Response 3:** "What are you planning to do about it?" This response shows your interest, which is good, but that *you* tends to tear down the rapport you've just begun to build. Think again:
>
> **Response 4:** "Well, what should we do about it?"

BACK TO YOU

By trading *you* for *we*, you convey the message that you are always thinking of the other person. This, in turn, invites the other person to reciprocate by thinking of you. Two people thinking of each other? That's "rapport" in a nutshell.

Building on the Foundation

The first-person plural pronouns are the verbal foundation of rapport. As with any other foundation, this one is intended to be built upon. Here is a selection of more helping words. Notice that they all convey or are compatible with the values of collaboration and cooperation:

brainstorm
collaborate
confer
cooperate
huddle
learn
listen
solve
team up
work together

Doubtless, you can extend this list considerably.

How to Wreck Rapport

While it's important to know how to build rapport, it's also essential to understand how rapport may be torn down.

Exclusionary Language

Remember, rapport is about joining together, so the destruction of rapport is about pulling apart; the surest way to wreck rapport is to use exclusionary language instead of inclusive language. Exclusionary language includes using *I*, *mine*, *you*, and *yours* instead of the inclusive plural pronouns *we*, *us*, *ours*. It also consists of words that negate, deny, contradict, reject, or refuse. Here are some examples:

afraid
bad luck
cannot
crisis
delay
fail
fault
fear
final
forgot
impossible
lose
nonnegotiable
stupid
tired

Exclusionary Behavior

Just as exclusionary language can wreck rapport, so can exclusionary behavior. Examples include:

- **Using inappropriate language.** Making off-color, tasteless, or thoughtless comments; telling rude jokes; and using inappropriate, unwelcome, or demeaning nicknames are all instances of language choices that constitute exclusionary behavior. (Inappropriate language can do more than wreck rapport. Off-color remarks, sexual innuendo, and the like may be legally interpreted as contributing to the creation of a "hostile work environment," exposing you and your company to civil and even possibly criminal liability.)

- **Habitual tardiness to appointments and meetings.** Being late broadcasts at least four messages, all of them destructive: you are disorganized, you are incompetent, you lack respect for others, and you just don't care.

- **Sloppy, inappropriate, or disrespectful dress or grooming.** Observe how others dress in your workplace. Emulate the standard that is set. Just because your firm does not have a formally stated dress code does not mean the company lacks a dress code. Look at the colleagues and bosses you most admire. *They* are your firm's dress code.

- **Bad telephone and email manners.** Habitual failure to pick up calls, failure to return calls, failure to take or relay messages, keeping callers on hold, starting to talk before the receiver is in position, eating while talking, mumbling, drifting off into inattention, and slamming down the phone—all of these are rapport wreckers. Lapses in email etiquette include failing to answer emails, forwarding emails the sender probably does not want to share with a wider audience, deluging others with nonessential emails, and writing illiterate emails (bad spelling, bad grammar, careless word choice).

- **Failure to greet people and to greet them warmly and appropriately.** We say a lot with our bodies, with our physical, nonverbal presence. A limp handshake is never welcome, but neither is a bonecrusher. Both transmit nonverbal messages that wreck rapport. Failure to look the other person in the eye is likewise off-putting. Frowns, hand-wringing, sighs—all of these gestures of anxiety tear down existing rapport or prevent the establishment of new rapport.

- **Failure to listen and/or failure to show that you are listening.** Making and maintaining eye contact in person-to-person conversation is critically important. Nod in agreement as you listen. Widen your eyes to show interest. Resist the temptation to interrupt. Ask relevant questions.

- **Intruding on another's space or privacy.** Fewer and fewer workplaces these days offer the "luxury" of individual offices with real walls and actual doors. Most of us inhabit cubicles. Treat your coworker's cubicle as if it were an office with a closed door. Don't barge in. Don't start talking without offering a greeting and making a request. As you stand *outside* of the cubicle, say, "Good morning, John." Then make your request: "Can I speak with you a moment?"

- **Generally swinish behavior.** This ranges from failure to replace the paper in the copier or printer to pilfering food others have stored in the break room fridge.

Creating the Right Feelings

The language of business, we've said more than once now, is money—money made and money saved. Your performance is measured first and last in hard numbers. Nevertheless, achieving these numbers is not strictly a matter of dollars and cents. Performance is also a function of consistently giving people the right feelings.

Greetings!

You don't have to be a motivational speaker or charismatic rock star to get folks to feel good about you. Giving people the right feelings is actually a simple and direct process.

Start each day off on a bright and positive note by saying *Good morning*. Do more. Add a name: "Good morning, Esther!" And if time permits, extend the greeting: "Good morning, Esther! How was your weekend?" When you can, make it more personal: "Good morning, Esther! How did that yard sale go on Saturday?"

The Territorial Imperative

Anthropologists have a name for the study of how we define and use our personal space. They call it *proxemics*. You don't have to earn a PhD in the subject to promote rapport by paying closer attention to how people treat their space. This is especially important in our cubicle-crowded era.

Make the most of the geography of the modern workplace. Complaining about your lousy cube will not enhance rapport; therefore, don't complain. Instead, do what you can to treat your cubicle as your office—and to treat the cubicles of others as *their* offices. This means that you should always respect the privacy of your colleagues, just as if they occupied an office with four real walls and a door. As already mentioned, don't barge in. Ask permission to enter. In addition:

- Never enter another person's cubicle if that person is not present, except to deliver something or leave a note.

- When you are scheduled to meet someone, wait outside the cubicle until its owner shows up for the meeting.

- When you are visiting someone's cubicle or office, ask permission before you rearrange the furniture: "Do you mind if I move this chair closer?"

- Pick up after yourself. Take your trash with you when you leave, including that ugly Styrofoam coffee cup.

- Don't put your coffee cup on a person's desk without asking permission. Regard the desk as the inner sanctum of the other person's territory. Respect it.

- Don't borrow stuff—staplers, pens, whatever—without permission. Be sure to return what you borrow.

- Never snoop or give the appearance of snooping. Resist the impulse to read what's on the other person's desk.

Just as you respect the territory of another, fashion your own space into a territory that commands respect. If you have a choice of office furniture, devote your most concentrated attention to your chair. Kings and queens occupy thrones because what we sit on transmits a powerful nonverbal message about the degree of power we possess.

- An expensive-looking chair brings to mind a throne. A cheap-looking chair brings to mind a footstool. Which one will you choose?

- A chair with armrests always looks more prestigious than a chair without armrests, which most people associate with secretaries and assistants, not executives.

- Arrange the furniture in your work space to enhance the perception of the amplitude and adequacy of the space. If possible, position your chair so that you can lean back without touching a wall or bookcase. Give the impression that you've got space to spare.

- Personalize your space with artwork you enjoy and pictures of your family. Just ensure that you follow company rules or policies governing the decoration of offices. While awards and certificates are always appropriate, avoid decorating with nude or suggestive artwork, political slogans, humorous material, off-color material, religious images, religious symbols, or religious texts. Anything with even a hint of a sexual connotation is to be avoided. Childish decorations—such as stuffed animals—and military memorabilia—especially weaponry—are to be avoided. Let this principle guide you: Everything you put in your office speaks for and about you, broadcasting not simply who you are, but who you think you are, and who you want others to think you are.

- Keep your work space neat and clean. Unless security and confidentiality are at issue, it is usually unnecessary to clear your desk every evening, but do keep it organized looking.

- Avoid inappropriate or questionable screensaver images for your computer. If your firm has a logo screensaver, use it.

Being a "nice guy" does not require you to surrender your personal space. Assert yourself, but do so calmly and pleasantly.

- When Joe "borrows" your stapler without returning it, ask for it back: "Joe, I need my stapler back, please."

- If you don't want people waiting in your office when you're not present, mention it both gently and straightforwardly: "Jack, next time you get here before I do, please wait outside."

Help: Offer and Ask

Not surprisingly, an offer of help is an efficient way to create rapport. But if you want to create rapport even more efficiently, don't offer help, *ask* for it. Asking for help empowers the other person, giving him powerfully good feelings about himself. Your request for assistance is, after all, a vote of confidence.

When you are asked for help, the only proper response is to give it. It does not matter if you are unable to give the requester all the help she needs. Do what you can, and if you can do nothing directly, you can still *help* her find someone who can help. "Alice, I've never used one of those machines, but Esther has. Let me get her on the phone for you."

In offering help, be proactive. Don't wait to be asked. When you see a coworker in need, request permission to be of service: "Bill, can I help you with that?" Don't risk embarrassing or belittling the other person with "You sure look like you can use some help" and similar phrases. Pass no judgment; just ask permission to help. Put it in the form of a question: "Can I help?"

When you need help, ask for it. But, before you do, take the necessary time and make the needed effort to identify the best sources of aid. Consider:

- Who does what job?

- Who commands influence and enjoys respect?

- Who is always in the loop?

- Who do others usually ask?

- Who makes the important decisions?

By answering these questions, you identify not only the people who have the greatest power to help you but also the people with whom it is always valuable to establish a connection.

The worst thing you can do when asking for help is to apologize for asking: "I'm sorry to bother you . . ." To avoid the temptation to apologize, stop thinking of your request as taking something and instead start thinking of it as giving something, namely the opportunity to be helpful. That is a valuable opportunity for the other person because it offers the prospect of empowerment and the good feelings that brings.

- If you need help immediately, say: "Tom, I need your help."

- If there is no urgency, cut the other person more slack: "Tom, I need your help with something. When's a good time to talk?"

- If there is truly no great hurry, approach even more casually: "Tom, mind if I pick your brain about something?"

- Don't dump your problem in someone else's lap. Be as specific as possible about the help you need and provide as much useful information as you can.

When you accept help, the only proper response is an expression of gratitude.

- A simple *thanks* may be sufficient, but it is even better to be more specific: "Thanks. You are saving me a lot of time."

- Never apologize: "I'm really sorry I had to bother you." This tells the person who has just spent time and effort helping you that she should feel annoyed or angry or irritated. What you really want her to feel is happy to have helped.

- Never belittle yourself: "I'm an idiot when it comes to these things." Do not plant a negative assessment of your competence or value to the organization. Bear in mind: Anything you say can be used against you.

Offer Praise and Offer Criticism

Much as asking for help creates even more rapport than offering help, so offering creative criticism can create at least as much rapport as giving unalloyed praise. Of course, it is easier to praise than to criticize, but offering genuinely constructive criticism often represents an even greater service.

As easy as it is to praise, do beware of possible pitfalls:

- Avoid the appearance of insincerity or sarcasm. Be wholly positive.

- Never patronize or talk down to a colleague or subordinate. Avoid expressing astonishment: "*You* did *this*! I'm amazed!"

- Avoid vagueness, which suggests insincerity. Be as specific as possible. Instead of saying "You're doing a wonderful job," say "Cutting turnaround time by half an hour really means a lot." Use nouns and verbs in preference to adjectives and adverbs.

- Avoid the appearance of sucking up to your boss. This is best done by congratulating him for specific achievements.

When you feel the need to offer criticism, take a breath. Pause. Do a rapid reality check before you speak:

1. Never criticize *anyone*. Address all of your remarks to an issue, a project, an action, or an outcome. Do not remark on a person, trait, attitude, or personality.

2. Before opening your mouth, make certain that the situation does indeed require criticism. Ask and answer: *Is this worth criticizing?*

3. Before criticizing, ask and answer whether the situation at issue can be improved or corrected. If the problem can't be fixed, hold your tongue.

4. Always ask permission before offering criticism. "Would you like to hear my take on this?"

5. Choose the right place and time. Never embarrass anyone by delivering criticism in front of others. Instead, make an appointment: "John, there's something I want to discuss with you. What would be a good time for you when we might have a few uninterrupted moments?"

6. Back up criticism with substance. Don't be vague. Cite specific problems, incidents, actions: "Mark, I'd like us all to be more proactive in offering help to customers. Next time you're on the sales floor, reach out to at least three customers by asking 'How may I help you?'"

7. Arm yourself with helpful alternatives. Never tear down without helping to build up: "This approach won't work for us because it takes too much time. Let's try this alternative . . ."

8. Adopt an informal, friendly tone. Do not use "command" language ("you must," "you have to," and so on): "I think you'll find it more effective to use the direct line, Rachel."

9. Temper criticism with praise, if possible. Avoid making the other person feel like a complete failure: "You've certainly solved the first two problems, but number three still isn't working. Let's review our options."

10. Don't overwhelm the person with serial criticisms. Identify and address one issue at a time. "The critical thing to get right is X. Once we've got that going, we can take care of everything else."

11. Don't hit and run. Follow up with positive feedback, including praise, congratulations, and thanks: "Bill, thanks for making those changes. They've made a real difference! We're up by at least 20 percent."

12. Don't make threats or dramatic predictions of dire consequences. This does not mean you should avoid discussing the consequences or possible consequences of whatever you are criticizing. Nor should you minimize or sugarcoat facts. Just be certain that you are being objective and factual. Always address issues, not egos: "We've still got problems with X, Y, and Z. Let's sit down and hash out the issues one by one."

Accepting Criticism

You may have to fight the urge to gag on the following advice, but it is valuable advice nevertheless: *Be grateful for criticism.*

First, the criticism may be genuinely useful and constructive, guiding you to improve a product, a situation, or your own skills. Second, even if the criticism is off-base and unfounded, the act of criticizing shows that the other person cares about what you are doing. You are having an effect. You are being recognized.

How you respond to criticism profoundly influences the way coworkers, subordinates, and bosses think about you. There are three natural impulses to understand and to resist:

1. The impulse to respond defensively and angrily.

2. The impulse to dig in and angrily refuse to listen.

3. The impulse to fold up and abandon all self-confidence.

Acting on any of these impulses is destructive of rapport. Prepare yourself instead to profit from criticism by adopting the attitude that it is a kind of gift, an opportunity to learn and to improve. It is useful and affirmative. Based on this attitude:

- **Listen.** Demonstrate that you are listening by using effective body language. Make and maintain eye contact with your critic. Suppress such signals of resistance as placing your hand over your mouth or on your forehead, as if to shade your eyes. Do not fold your arms across your chest—a gesture that always telegraphs defiance.

- **Ask questions.** Ask for advice.

- **Thank your critic.**

Listening not just politely but carefully to criticism is *not* the same as agreeing with the criticism. Just as it is important to resist the impulse to deny out of hand the validity of the criticism, so it is destructive simply to surrender to it, to take a critical remark as the gospel truth. Criticism is a perception. Listen, think, then explore—with yourself and with the critic—the substance on which the criticism is based.

If you conclude that the criticism is indeed unfounded, resist the impulse to respond in anger or with irritation and impatience. Even if the criticism has little or no merit in objective fact, it tells you something about how you are putting yourself, your ideas, and your projects across. Perhaps you need to find ways to create more positive perceptions.

Friction and Conflict

Some workplaces are generally pleasant and smooth running, whereas others are continually plagued by friction and conflict. Most operate somewhere between these extremes. Whatever the climate in your shop, irritation, anger, and disputes happen. Like any other aspect of working life, they need to be managed—not ignored, not banished, not denied, but managed.

The very first decision to make is whether the emotion you feel is worth acting on in any way. The truth is that most causes of anger and irritation quickly pass. Don't ignore your feelings, but, if you can, follow the FIDO formula:

Forget It. Drive On.

Since most annoyances are transitory, why act in ways that tend to enshrine them with destructive permanence?

This said, not all episodes of anger and annoyance can pass the FIDO test. If a *situation* is making your work life miserable or interfering with your productivity or that of the organization, it is time to act. Before you do, however, note the use of the word *situation* in the preceding sentence. That word is, of course, by no means synonymous with *person.* You may feel anger or irritation toward another person, but it is almost always a mistake to address those emotions in terms of that individual's personality. Whereas situations can be changed—can be fixed—people are not so readily fixable.

When you address the sources of friction, keep the conversation low-key. Just as when you deliver constructive criticism, focus on the situation, the issues, the actions, the behavior, rather than on personalities. And, when you address the issue, do so in private and at a low volume. By all means, express your feelings—how the situation affects you and the work you do—but speak in a normal conversational tone. Don't tell the person how he or she is making you feel. Instead, focus on the issue for which the person is responsible and explain how that *issue* makes you feel: "Bob, when you took credit for the widget idea, I really felt hurt."

Situations that generate irritation and anger are most effectively resolved by replacing these unpleasant and potentially destructive emotions with rapport. Your object in talking to the other person is not to win by defeating him. Instead, your goal should be to create empathy, to make the *other* person see reality from *your* perspective. If you succeed in doing this, you will probably receive an apology, which you should then accept gracefully and in a few well-chosen words. If possible, look toward the future: "Thanks, Bob. I appreciate your apology, and I understand that you didn't mean to cut me out of the loop. What you said will make it easier for us to continue to do great things with the project."

Address issues, not egos. Create empathy. If you can do this, you will resolve workplace anger on most occasions. It is possible, especially in anxious times, that a situation will escalate, and if you ever feel that emotions are getting out of hand—your emotions or those of the other person—the most effective step you can take is a step back and away. Don't turn your back, and don't run. But just as it takes two to collaborate, it takes two to argue. Therefore, remove yourself from the equation. "Bob, this is getting too hot. I'll be back in about half an hour. Let's see if we can take this up more productively then."

The problem with engaging in angry disputes is that, no matter who is finally judged right or wrong (and there may never be a definitive judgment), *you* are becoming connected with a source of unproductive distraction. This guilt by association makes you appear to be anything but indispensable. If you cannot quietly *resolve* the situation, *interrupt* the situation by withdrawing. Do not gossip about the angry exchange to others. Nevertheless, if you feel physically threatened, not only should you remove yourself from the presence of the other person, you should also talk to a supervisor or, if necessary, Security.

Apologies That Build Rapport

No one likes to say *I'm sorry*. This would seem self-evident, but, actually, it's not. The truth is that it's not the apology we dread, but the sharp pain or dull ache of having made the mistake that necessitates the apology.

Don't like to apologize? Stop making mistakes.

But, of course, we all make mistakes. And, so, apologies will, from time to time, be necessary. Why not make the most out of them?

The constructive approach to apology is to begin by accepting the precipitating incident—the error, the misstep—as a fact. There was an egg. Now it is broken. Having accepted this, look upon the *necessary* apology as an *opportunity*. How you respond to "your bad" can go a long way toward building and strengthening workplace rapport.

Here is how it works: If, as the saying goes, to err is human and to forgive divine, every time you err, you present others with an opportunity to forgive—that is, to act in a godlike manner. Managed correctly, an apology will ease your guilt, even as it makes the person to whom you apologize feel downright good.

For an apology to be productive, it must be timely. When something goes wrong, don't wait to be asked for an explanation. Be proactive. Offer an apology together with an explanation. The timely apology must also be genuinely helpful. If it's a good thing to say that you're sorry, it's far better to follow up with a solution, a remedy, or at the very least an offer of help. Thus, an effective apology has four components:

1. The part most of us think of as the apology itself: Saying you are sorry.

2. An embrace of responsibility: You take ownership of your error.

3. An expression of empathy: You understand the other person's feelings.

4. An offer of a remedy or promise that you will help the other person resolve the situation: Do what you can to create rapport by moving the conversation from *I* and *you* to *we* and *us*.

Here is an example:

You: Ted, I apologize for being late with that data update. I understand I put you in an uncomfortable situation. I'm sorry.

Ted: Well, the boss wasn't very happy with me.

You: I bet you were ticked off about that. I'm going to meet with the boss now, and I'll explain what happened. I didn't get the update on the first three tests on time. I don't know if I could have done anything about that, but I certainly should have alerted you. I didn't mean to leave you blindsided like that. I'll let him know what happened.

Ted: I'd appreciate that. Thanks.

The tone is sincere without being dramatic. Remember that the apology is about the *other* person's feelings, not about yours. Saying "I feel awful about this" is *not* going to make the other person feel any better. In fact, an expression of your discomfort may add the emotion of guilt to the other person's freight of unpleasant feelings. Keep the apology objective, but add the element of empathy right away, quickly followed by an offer of remedy.

Commemorate and Celebrate

Few workplaces ever feel like home, nor should they; however, the most productive workplaces do feel like a community—a place of collaborative rapport. If you take responsibility for enhancing this feeling, you will not only improve the productivity of the workplace, you will also draw attention to yourself as someone who is at the emotional center of the community. You don't have to be inherently charismatic or a "born leader" to achieve this. All that is required is taking the time and effort to learn something about the special days in the lives of your colleagues, subordinates, and bosses.

Why not appoint yourself as the person responsible for keeping track of birthdays, employment anniversaries, and the like? Take charge of this position by sending an email invitation to everyone in your department or work group to acknowledge John's tenth anniversary with the firm, or Zara's birthday. Also be the one who sends the email announcing a birth, a graduation—any important event that is generally shared among members of a community.

Be sensitive to the climate in your office. You want to be a source of community feeling, not the jerk who disrupts work several times a week to celebrate this or that. Look for ways to incorporate the daily routine into the celebration of special events. Everyone's got to eat lunch, right? You might be the person who gets everyone together to take Sally out for lunch when she returns from maternity leave.

You can also appoint yourself as the person in charge of collecting money for an office gift on the occasion of Jack's tenth anniversary with the department. Just be certain to present this as an *opportunity* for people to contribute, and not as a demand for cash. Also be aware of your company's policies regarding solicitation of money among employees. Some firms prohibit it for *any* reason. Don't break the rules even for a "good cause."

Communities come together to mourn as well as to celebrate. When a coworker suffers a loss, be certain to express your condolences personally. You may find this difficult. Perhaps you are afraid that you will intrude on someone's grief. Be assured, however, that acknowledging the loss will not be seen as an intrusion, but will be welcomed. The grief of loss is lonely. Your words will make it a less solitary experience.

Whereas you may appoint yourself the unofficial office celebrator, you do not want to become known as the office ghoul, who always broadcasts bad or sad news. Nevertheless, if your coworker tells you about a loss, a generous and rapport-building response is to ask permission to let others know: "Pete, I'm so sorry for your loss. Would you like me to let the others know? I can circulate an email." If Pete wants you to do this, ask him if there is any information he would like you to pass along. For example, some families ask that donations be made to a charitable cause in lieu of sending cards or flowers.

When a bereaved coworker returns to the office, express your empathy simply and directly. "Pete, I'm so sorry for your loss" is always appropriate, but if you were acquainted with the deceased, even slightly, it is very helpful to add a personal detail that focuses on the life lived rather than on the life lost. "Pete, I'm so sorry for your loss. You know, I met your mother only that one time she visited the office, but it was apparent what a wonderful lady she was." Offer help: "If there's anything I can do for you, please ask, okay?"

Courtesy: Common and Uncommon

This chapter has been about building a rapport that connects you with your workplace—your colleagues, subordinates, and bosses—in a variety of positive ways. It's about being liked and valued, not just for who you are, but for what your presence means to the working community of which you are a part. As we have seen, most of this rapport-building enterprise is actually quite easy to carry out. At bottom, it calls for practicing what people typically call "common courtesy." But when you go the extra mile to ensure that *common* courtesy prevails in your workplace, that valuable commodity is raised to the next level. The people around you don't take it for granted. Instead, they take note, and, in this way, "common" courtesy is raised to a level that seems, well, downright *uncommon*. Associate yourself with this, and your own perceived value to the workplace community will rise accordingly to an "uncommon" level. And that is exactly where you want it to be.

CHAPTER 6

FROM OFFICE POLITICS TO OFFICE DIPLOMACY

To be called a skilled office politician is not necessarily a compliment. Many people associate "office politics" with amoral or downright unethical manipulation, as well as with conniving, sucking up, and occasionally inserting a knife in an unsuspecting back. The best move is to take a step beyond office politics and enter office diplomacy. This chapter shows you how to rise from *office politician*—one who knows how to manipulate others to get ahead—to *office diplomat*: the team player who brings the team together, who keeps the team together, and who positions the team to win. This often requires you to take charge, even if "supervisor," "manager," or "director" isn't part of your official job title. As you will see, taking charge does not mean barking out orders. It does mean encouraging and guiding people toward the *productive* resolution of conflict. This is the essence of office diplomacy, and if you practice it both effectively and consistently, you will find yourself actually climbing the ladder to those rungs reserved for *supervisors*, *managers*, and *directors*.

Conflict: Not Bad, Not Good, Just Is

If the phrase "office politics" gets a bad rap, "friction" and "conflict" suffer even more unfairly. For the mechanically inclined, *friction* means the thing that wears out machinery, and if you're just a guy trying to get along, *conflict* is the factor that keeps life from running smoothly. But if you can set aside semantic prejudice, consider that, for all the inconvenience they often cause, both *friction* and *conflict* are absolutely necessary. We could not do without them.

The Effects of Friction

Begin with friction. Take it away, and you couldn't get anywhere—your feet would slip without propelling you, and if you had wheels, they'd spin but get you nowhere. And if you ever somehow managed to get going, you could never stop—until something stopped you. And that something would probably be quite hard.

The word *friction* serves double duty in English, describing what happens when physical bodies rub up against each other and also what happens when conflicting thoughts, motives, goals, wants, desires, or personalities figuratively do the same. Friction, in this sense, is the product of conflict and, in turn, generates more conflict.

We like to think of friction and the conflict associated with it as the unfortunate accidents of business life. We like to think that a "normal" or "routine" business day is one that goes *smoothly*, and that days marked by friction and conflict are aberrations and exceptions. The fact is, however, that friction and conflict are regular, and quite necessary, features of workplace physics: not bad, not good, just is.

Stop Blaming and Start Managing

Workplace friction is a product of conflict and, in turn, creates conflict. It is a lot like mechanical friction, which can slowly wear down the moving parts of a machine or suddenly jam up the works altogether, sometimes with catastrophic results. In the workplace, friction and conflict may wear people down over time, may reduce the speed and efficiency with which jobs get done, may make even the most routine processes more difficult and burdensome, and may cause everything to grind to a sudden halt or, worse yet, generate sufficient heat to cause an explosion.

None of these outcomes is desirable, but don't blame friction and conflict for them. They're inevitable. Instead, start devoting attention to how you manage friction and conflict. Just bear in mind the usefulness of friction in the physical world. It keeps us from slipping and allows us to move ahead. Similarly, in business or other organized endeavors, conflict provides the friction that permits us to advance. As an office diplomat, your objective should not be to eliminate conflict—an impossible task in any case—but to manage it effectively. As General George S. Patton Jr. liked to say, "If everybody is thinking the same way, nobody is thinking." Minimize conflict where its presence is nonproductive, but make good use of it where it generates a multiplicity of useful ideas and produces a variety of approaches.

The Roots of Conflict

Some people believe that conflict is so pervasive that it can be generated whenever two people disagree. Sound extreme? Actually, it's not extreme enough. Haven't you ever argued with yourself? The truth is that conflict can occur even when you are all alone: "I debated with myself for a half hour whether to choose Option A or Option B, and I'm still not sure I made the right decision." Typically, however, conflict happens whenever two or more people disagree on how to handle a situation.

How Conflict Becomes Destructive

Because different people think and feel differently, and because the needs and wants of different people vary, it is unreasonable to expect perfect agreement in every situation. Fortunately, multiple perspectives have great value; therefore, when you set out to manage conflict, do not make your goal the elimination of disagreement. Instead, endeavor to prevent disagreement from becoming destructive. Begin by considering the most likely causes of harmful escalation:

- **Situations with a lot at stake.** It is quite possible to disagree over what flavor doughnuts should be ordered for the break room in the morning, but it is highly unlikely that tempers will flare in the course of this debate. But when the company has funds to hire just three new assistants and there are four of you competing for them, the outbreak of a destructive conflict becomes a distinct possibility.

- **Crises.** Revenue has crashed, department budgets have been slashed. The office is in crisis mode. What this comes down to is a sharp reduction in the room to maneuver. It is a situation that makes people feel trapped, and, trapped, some people respond in a panic-driven, irrational, highly defensive, turf-protecting, angry way. The potential for an explosive conflict rises.

- **Personal differences.** Some people just don't get along with each other. It's that old oil-and-water thing. Forced to work with someone you don't like, you could just fight or give up in despair. The better alternative is to find a way around the conflict.

- **Conflicting goals, needs, or wants.** No one can escape the Principle of Scarcity: a multitude of needs and wants versus a shortage of resources to satisfy them all. Marketing clamors for more ad dollars, while R&D wants to boost its research and development budget. Who gets the money?

It is especially crucial to manage conflict effectively in these high-risk categories. The goal is not to manage it to death, but to make productive use of it.

Learning to Value Conflict

The first step in managing conflict is to learn to value conflict. While you should work toward agreement—a significant level of consensus—on all disputed issues, do not reject the value of multiple perspectives, interpretations, assessments, and opinions. Your objective is to elicit a productive decision. Conflict, varied opinion, and argument are all valid vehicles for arriving at that decision. Therefore, when conflict comes about, resist your natural urge to respond negatively to it, to attempt to nip it in the bud, to deny it, to stifle it, to ignore it, to scold people for arguing, or to browbeat one person into surrendering to the point of view of another. Instead, welcome conflict, and then manage it by:

- Inviting all concerned parties to present their points of view in full and without interruption.

- Encouraging frank discussion and free debate.

- Focusing all attention and discussion on facts and issues rather than on personalities.

- Reassuring all concerned parties that debate and disagreement are creative: "I feel as if we're really getting somewhere."

- Thanking everyone for his or her good ideas: "Ed, I never looked at it that way. What you said really makes me think."

- Reinforcing a commitment to collaboration and team effort by reminding those involved that everyone is working toward a solution to a problem in which everyone has a stake.

Know When to Be a Coach, and Know When to Be a Referee

Encouraging others to value conflict requires the mentality of a coach, a combination cheerleader, mentor, and taskmaster. But when conflict threatens to become divisive and destructive, you need to be both sufficiently aware and sufficiently nimble to shift rapidly from coach to referee. This may require, first and foremost, that you exercise self-control to prevent getting sucked into a heated conflict yourself.

The key is to avoid responding emotionally to rapidly unfolding events. It would be convenient if we could always successfully remind ourselves to think before giving in to our emotions, but in the grip of a high-stakes situation, it is all too easy to be overwhelmed. You can, however, take proactive steps to help prevent this.

Now—or as soon as possible—when you are sitting alone and calm in your office or cubicle, look around you. Let your eyes light on some object on your desk. It doesn't much matter what the object is, as long as it is always reliably there, on your desk. Tell yourself, out loud, that whenever you sense that you are about to react out of pure feeling—to respond without thinking—*that* object will be your reminder to stop, to listen silently to the other person or persons, and to think. Only then will you respond, and when you respond, it will be to discuss the matter at issue, not the personalities of those involved in a burgeoning conflict.

There need not be anything special about your chosen object. It is special only because you have chosen it as your aid to remembering how to act and how not to act. Veteran management writer Dean H. Shapiro Jr. advised back in 1978 (in his *Precision Nirvana*) that you can also choose something to carry in your pocket at all times, not just when you are seated at your desk. His idea was to tote around the kind of counter golfers use to keep their score. Whenever you're tempted to flare up in knee-jerk emotion, click the counter instead. The advantage of carrying your reminder with you is that it is always with you, and since destructive conflict can erupt anytime and anywhere, this may be a very good way to nudge you out of coaching mode and onto the referee track when necessary.

Stop Defending Yourself

Before you can be an effective referee, you need to know the single most important rule of the game: *First open up, then stay open.*

Business can be highly competitive, and for many of us, our first impulse is to hang on to whatever we've got and defend it with a vengeance, whether it's a stapler on our desk or an idea we've just presented.

The problem with acting on this protective impulse is that your defense may mean closing yourself off to opinions, ideas, or points of view that challenge yours. While it may be necessary to explain, clarify, and even to justify your statements and positions, it is never necessary—or desirable—to explain and justify them by refusing to hear and consider what others have to say. The strength of a group enterprise is in its diversity of perspective, brain, and heart. You should try to benefit from, not automatically reject, this multiplication of analytical and inventive power. When Sonya suggests an approach that differs from yours, thank her for it and give it full consideration: "Sonya, thanks. I haven't thought about the problem this way. Give me some time to think about your approach, and let's discuss it further."

Once you overcome your own defensive impulses, intervene, as the alert referee you should be, to curb the excessive defensiveness of others.

Hank presents Idea A. Mary offers Idea B:

Hank: Mary, I've just explained how Idea A addresses all the issues. Let's get moving on it, huh?

You: Hold on a minute, Hank. I would like to hear what Mary has to say about Idea B. You've identified the major issues very thoroughly, Hank, and I believe we'd benefit from taking a look at just how Idea B would tackle them. You've put so much effort into defining the problems. Let's take a little more time to consider all the alternatives.

Hank is already acting on his defensive impulse, so you'd better not engage him as an opponent but approach him instead as an ally. Acknowledge and praise the good work he has done, then suggest that Mary's idea may add value to Hank's investment of time and effort. Building on one proposal does not necessarily require tearing down another.

Conflict Management Procedures

Since workplace conflict can assault the emotions, which, in turn, may overwhelm the rational thought process, the most effective approach to managing such conflict is to apply modest but systematic procedures to separate issues from feelings, address those issues, and, by doing this effectively, give everyone the feelings you want them to have.

Slap a Label on It

In business, emotions can run high. When they're good feelings that drive enthusiasm, the results can be splendid. When, however, they're feelings born of anxiety and sheer defensiveness, they cloak the useful and necessary elements, a thorough knowledge of issues, objectives, and consequences, in a dense fog. Clear the air by identifying the issues:

- Use that object on your desk or in your pocket to remind you to think before you react emotionally.

- Having reminded yourself to think, actually start thinking. Define the conflict and the elements of the conflict. What is it really about? What are the substantive *issues*—not feelings—driving the conflict?

- Give each issue a name, a label. Make a list of all the labels, and be as specific as possible. Some people think of lists as the dullest kind of writing possible, but, actually, there is a very real magic about making a list. It makes the fog disappear.

Share your list-making enterprise. Donning your referee hat, say to the other person or to the group, "Hold on. Before we start going in a bunch of different directions, let's take an inventory of just exactly what issues are in play here. Alice, why don't you go first? What do you see as the main problems?"

Make it your responsibility to write down the responses, to compile the list as each of the others speaks his or her piece. Give everyone a turn, and let each person speak without interruption. If José breaks in on Alice, intervene: "José, let's let Alice list all the issues that concern her, then we'll turn to you and the others. It will be easier to discuss and evaluate the problem if we get everything out into the open first. I promise you, we will talk about everything that concerns you. But let's get it all out first."

Choose Your Battles Carefully

Successful generals walk away from as many battles as they fight. They understand that the commander who chooses the time and place of a battle instead of having the battle thrust upon him enjoys a great tactical and strategic advantage. Emulate the victorious and memorize this sentence: *You do not have to fight every battle.*

It is true that some conflicts cannot or should not be dodged. When you believe your team is about to choose a destructive course of action, now is not the time to walk away. Raise objections and offer alternatives. If doing so means a dispute, take the necessary steps to help make that dispute productive, but know that it is a battle worth fighting. Nevertheless, don't assume that you are obliged to intervene in *every* conflict that comes your way. Before you engage, ask and answer six questions for yourself:

1. Are the issues and possible or likely outcomes worth expending energy on?

2. Are the issues and possible or likely outcomes worth putting goodwill at risk?

3. Has the other person or group made a decision? And if so, is the decision subject to review or change?

4. What will happen if the other person or group wins? Can you live with the consequences? Can you (in the words of the cliché) squeeze lemonade from the lemons?

5. If you choose not to fight and instead let the other person win now, will this give you tangible bargaining chips for the future?

6. Does *this* problem have to be solved at *this* time? There is a downside to putting off discussions, debates, and disputes, but the fact is

that some should be put off in order to address more pressing issues. Make a judgment call. If a dispute promises to be contentious, requiring significant time and energy to resolve, decide if the investment of resources has to be made now and at the expense of other, higher-priority projects. In other words, prioritize.

Neither Offer nor Accept an Invitation to an Ambush

The rewards of "gotcha" are illusory. Ambush a colleague, and you might feel the momentary satisfaction of vengeance, but you may also sow the seeds of long-term conflict.

Workplace conflict should never be permitted to become a spectator sport. Do not ignore disputes that cry out for resolution, but do whatever is necessary to arrange for a discussion of contentious matters in private or in the presence of a manager and at a time that everyone involved finds convenient.

Don't Multitask Disputes

Multitasking is expected in today's workplace, where the emphasis is on individual productivity and where becoming indispensable is often mostly about doing even more than is expected. But hashing out disputes should be declared strictly off-limits to multitasking.

Do not cluster complaints and accusations. Instead, prioritize the issues at dispute. Address the most pressing first—those whose resolution will allow you and your group to exploit an opportunity or prevent a catastrophe. Then go on to those most likely to be satisfactorily resolved. Having prioritized, focus on one high-priority issue at a time. Take ownership of each issue and do not move on to the next until the current one is resolved.

When multiple issues unavoidably present themselves simultaneously, begin by separating them, so that you can deal with each in serial fashion. Trying to attack a vague cluster of conflicts will likely produce only confusion and therefore amplify aggravation.

Be Specific and Speak Precisely

Emotion cannot be expected to produce precision. Pressured and frustrated, people typically lump what should be well-defined disputed issues into some vague category or accusation, such as "You never come in at budget!"

To declare that blanket statements are never true would be to issue a blanket statement. Nevertheless, such statements are rarely the whole truth, and even when they do express a significant part of the truth, blanket indictments are more provocative than helpful.

Set out to fix problems, not personalities. The most effective responses in a dispute resolve the conflict by satisfactorily addressing the underlying issues. If your car won't start in the morning, you can scream, cry, and complain, all of which address your feelings and may even make you feel better, but none of which will address the underlying issues, which may require seeking a jump start, a new battery, or a tow to the garage. Similarly, a vague complaint may get some aggravation off your chest, but it will do nothing about the sources of the aggravation.

Break your complaint down into its component parts. Be specific about sources of conflict. "The XYZ project did not come in on budget, which was the same problem you had with the ABC project two months ago. Before then, you were quite good at hitting your numbers. Let's meet to review your P&L projections for the last three quarters. Maybe we can track the source of the overruns."

By digging down to specifics, you not only reduce the negative emotional impact of a conflict, but you begin doing the work necessary to resolve the conflict at its sources. How much of the necessary work begins with definition? Probably 50 percent—and maybe even more, since the process of carefully describing a problem often in itself suggests solutions to the problem.

Argue with Your Ears

Begin by defining what it means to "win" an argument. *Hint:* Put the emphasis on "win." Just proving yourself right and the other person wrong isn't much of a victory, whereas resolving the argument by coming up with a solution that adds to the bottom line of the enterprise is a big, big win. You have the best chance of winning in this way if you let everyone have a say while successfully resisting the often powerful urge to interrupt.

Arguments are most effectively resolved and converted into enduring benefit through listening and then responding to what you've heard.

The Musketeer Solution

Even if you've never read Alexandre Dumas's celebrated novel or have never seen the gazillion movies based on it, you probably know the motto of the Three Musketeers: *All for one, one for all!*

It should be the core belief of every collaborative enterprise.

For, in the end, no one wins unless the enterprise itself wins. The workplace cannot thrive as an arena in which people play a zero-sum game, a contest in which one person can win only if another loses. There is but a single boat, and we are all in it. For this reason, as soon as you have defined the conflict, start shifting the discussion from areas of disagreement to areas of agreement. Find the common ground on which to build a common solution that will benefit the workplace community of which you are a member and want to remain a member. Identify yourself as a faithful steward of the company, and your bosses will be hard-pressed to find a reason to let you go.

Exploit Agreement, Transform Disagreement

It works like this:

- Once you have staked out areas of agreement, start working within those areas. Build what everyone can agree on.

- Having made a start by creating something positive, you have given everyone involved a stake in the successful resolution of the conflict.

- The next step is to venture out into the remaining areas of disagreement. Discuss what is working and what is not working—"We agree that the project is feasible, but we need more data. Harry, that's your area. Can you get us the additional data?"

  - *We agree that the project is feasible:* That's the part that is working.

  - *But we need more data:* This is the part that's not working.

  - *Harry, that's your area. Can you get us the additional data?* This is the path toward pushing the "not working" bit into the "is working" category.

Agree on an Action Plan

How will you travel the path you have laid out from "not working" to "is working"? Agree on an action plan.

What does Harry need to do to get the necessary additional data? And how will the rest of the group help him get it?

- List the tasks that need to be done.

- Assign everyone a well-defined task.

- Clearly define objectives, goals, measurable performance criteria, and timetables for each task.

- Make sure that you get buy-in from management for the solutions you reach.

Do the Executive Thing

Whatever your official job title, the office diplomat behaves like an executive—in the root sense of the word. That is, at its root, the job of an *executive* is to *execute*. To be recognized as an effective office diplomat, you must do more than merely broker the resolution of conflict. You must *execute* the results of your brokering by following through. Collaborative agreement and action plans are essential, but they are valueless without adequate execution.

People who are good at follow-through understand the meaning of the sentence *We're not finished yet.* When the meeting breaks up with everyone smiling—or at least no longer snarling at one another—your job isn't done. Now assume responsibility for writing the email memo that summarizes and outlines the action plan, including all assignments, personnel, performance criteria, and deadlines. Within the span of the deadlines agreed to, monitor progress on an ongoing basis. Encourage, cajole, nag, and goad as required.

Part of follow-through may be follow-up progress meetings, discussions, or reports. If aspects of the resolution have to be altered, adjusted, or renegotiated, be sure everyone recognizes the collective investment all of you have in the process. Remain open to suggestions and new ideas. Avoid expressing anything that smacks of exasperation. Keep the tone cooperative and upbeat by marking the progress you are making together. "We've come a long way. Last month we were arguing with one another, and now we're two steps from completion of a project that will mean a lot to this company and to every one of us." Sure, it's early, but start celebrating.

CHAPTER 7

BE THE "GO-TO" BRAND

The United States Bureau of Labor Statistics publishes a "National Employment Matrix," which (as of 2010) provided statistics and projections for 750 positions in 276 industries. No wonder the question "What business are you in?" can produce such a wide variety of responses. In the end, however, one response has universal application. Whether you work under A for the Accommodations industry, W for Wood Product Manufacturing, or any of the other 274 industries in between (the Matrix lists nothing under X, Y, or Z), your job comes down to selling.

Selling is the business of all business, and it is the job of everyone who works. You may actually sell hotel rooms or crown molding, or you may be an accountant for a hotel chain or the assistant manager of a lumberyard, but, first and last, you still sell. You sell your value to your industry, to your firm, to your department, to your colleagues, to your bosses. If you stop selling or if you fail to sell, you may lose an opportunity, a promotion, or perhaps a stake in the future of your career. More immediately, you may lose your job.

On a hot summer afternoon, when you're a ten-year-old kid with the only lemonade stand on the block, you don't have to do much to move your wares. But when competition appears down the street, you'd better figure out a way to set your merchandise apart from the other guy's. That, of course, is what branding is all about. Savvy merchandisers invest time, talent, and cash to create a brand for their product—a means of endowing it with an identity or a personality that excites consumers and potential consumers. A successful brand encapsulates a set of information, values, and expectations associated with a given product. Done right, branding makes selling much easier, especially against competing products. Consumers become loyal to a brand. The brand gives them confidence in the product and other positive feelings about the value it offers.

It does not take a vast leap of intellect and imagination to conclude that if branding has proved essential in selling laundry soap and deodorant, it can also be helpful in selling just about anything—including your value to your industry, firm, and department. This chapter is about tactics for branding yourself indispensable.

1. Be the Eternally Brand-New Brand

"Branding" merchandise involves a lot more than slapping a label on a box, but the label is certainly part of the brand, and marketers take great care in choosing the words they put on it. Common sense would tell us that the most powerful word you can attach to a product is *free*, and tests confirm that it is indeed a powerful word. Nevertheless, there is one word that trumps even *free*. It is *new.*

Marketing studies repeatedly demonstrate that consumers are drawn to any product that boasts a claim of "new." The concept has universal appeal. So why not apply it to branding *your* brand?

Make no mistake, employers need, want, and reward experience, including experience with their own company. But experience perpetually vies with novelty and freshness for attention. Fortunately, because you are a living, breathing, thinking human being rather than a day-old loaf of bread, you can brand your experienced self as new just about every day.

Offer the Latest

Be the person who comes up with fresh approaches to routine issues, problems, and processes. Keep up with the latest developments in your field or industry. Bring them up. Think of ways to apply them.

Be the chief source of news in your office. Read company and industry publications and cruise the web for developments relevant to your business. Share them right away. Discuss the latest.

Deliver Well-Seasoned Newness

If you've been around for a while, brand yourself as a winning combination of seasoned experience and fresh outlook. Federal law prohibits employment discrimination based on a worker's age, but don't kid yourself: Older workers must often combat the perception that they're not pulling their weight. Younger employees may see senior workers as "grandfathered in" or as short-timers marking the days to retirement and a pension.

Use these perceptions to your advantage. By thinking in fresh ways and advocating innovation, you will confound the cliché of the veteran employee. In this way and against this background, you can come across as vigorous, youthful, and innovative. At the same time, you can continue to make use of all that your experience has bought you:

- Genuine know-how.

- The wisdom that comes with having tried and evaluated many approaches and processes over the years.

- Seasoned judgment.

- A deep network of professional contacts within the company, within the industry, and among clients and customers.

Even as you promote new and improved approaches to the processes and problems you know well, work your network and do what you can to revive and reinforce existing bonds with longtime advocates. And never stop expanding that network. When times are hard, rally the troops. Voice your faith in the firm. Brand the company in much the same way as you brand yourself—as a combination of experience and innovation. Take younger coworkers out to lunch or coffee. Be seen with them. Treat them as equals. Show your interest in them and in their ideas.

Get Hired Every Day

Whether you are a longtime employee or a newcomer, one of the most effective tactics for keeping your brand fresh and "new" is to think of every day at your current job as an employment interview. Recall what you did to get yourself hired a month ago, a year ago, or a decade or more ago. More than likely, the catalytic ingredients in your interview were excitement, passion, and a promise to deliver a great product. Think about this daily. Relive the interview. Try to feel some of those old feelings. Then apply them to your present workday.

2. Be the Problem-Solver Brand

Everyone is in the selling business. Ultimately, your merchandise consists of your value to your employer and, most immediately, to your boss. That value may be defined in hundreds, even thousands of ways, depending on your specific job description. But, once again, there is a single job description that is universal. Every employer intends to hire—and every boss wants to have—problem solvers.

Problem solver is the one position that can never be filled redundantly. No organization has too many problem solvers, and virtually every organization wants more.

Your job may, in fact, be all about solving problems. If your job puts you in charge of balancing inventory against demand, it is up to you on a daily basis to solve the problem of avoiding surpluses while also preventing shortages. If you are a customer service rep, your problem is to solve the countless problems customers bring you. Problem solving is the essence of many jobs. But even if problem solving is not your stated duty, it will always be recognized, appreciated, and rewarded.

Bosses, managers, and colleagues typically have a lot of administrative and routine duties that compete with one another on a daily basis. Speed bumps, pitfalls, obstacles, and snafus rob everyone of valuable time. When you encounter a problem, resist the temptation to pass it along to someone else. Take the initiative. Do something about it. Succeed in solving or even minimizing it, and your boss or colleague will be grateful. Even if you cannot resolve the difficulty, chances are that your efforts to do so will be appreciated.

Seek Problems, Don't Hide from Them

As you work, you will likely encounter chronic, recurrent problems or routine processes that are clogged by inefficiencies. Decide to tackle these. Create solutions and improvements that streamline routines and make them more efficient. Introduce the solutions to your boss. Promote them. Establish your ongoing credentials as a problem solver.

Be Low-Maintenance

As important as it is to brand yourself as one who solves problems, it is even more critical that you avoid branding yourself as a high-maintenance employee—a *creator* of problems. Nobody likes incompetence, of course, but even if you are a top performer, you can still be perceived as a source of problems if you behave like a prima donna or a pain in the—well, you fill in the body part.

MULTIPLE CHOICE POP QUIZ

Most employees are fired . . .

A. Because they cannot do the job for which they were hired.

B. Because they lack the basic requisite skills.

C. Because they fall below some minimum productivity requirement.

D. Because they prove themselves to be high-maintenance.

The answer, as if you haven't guessed, is D.

A high-maintenance employee may be one who requires constant supervision and instruction. Obviously, such staffers are drains on the time and effort of others. But also falling under the high-maintenance umbrella are complainers, people who squawk about the size and location of their cubicle, who complain about too much or too little air-conditioning, who scream bloody murder when their computer runs too slow, who demand to be listened to as they discourse endlessly on irrelevant matters, and who are generally "difficult." The language of business, we have said repeatedly, is money—dollars made, dollars saved—and yet a great many firing decisions, probably the majority of them, are formulated on a subjective basis. No boss will ever say this out loud, but she's almost certainly thinking it: *I fired him because I just don't like him.*

Brand yourself as a problem solver, not a problem maker, and your boss will almost certainly become loyal to your brand.

3. Be the Clutch Brand

The Principle of Scarcity—apparently unlimited human wants and needs existing in a world of limited resources—is the fundamental economic problem and therefore is the foundation of the science of economics. No business, no matter how prosperous, is immune from this principle. Time, money, and other resources are never limitless. More often than not, they seem at best barely adequate to meet whatever demands are being made.

For most businesses, time, more than money, is the shortage that is both most chronic and most acute. That is why the word *deadline* sounds so dire. It conveys a serious message: Work that is late is value that is lost.

Brand yourself as the clutch player—the person who brings the work in on time, who can be relied on to make, if not beat, difficult deadlines. Be the hero.

Recall from Chapter 4 the distinction between promoting your "features" as an employee and your "benefits." Features are your skills and professional qualifications, whereas benefits are how your application of those features makes your boss (and others) feel. Decide to be the departmental clutch player—the person who consistently brings the project in on time, on budget, and with success—and you will create the kind of feelings your bosses will want to have all the time. Such feelings will make them want the benefits you offer today, tomorrow, and far into the future.

The clutch player is the indispensable player: the man or woman the team can always count on. Conversely, to the extent that you fail to meet deadlines and overcome difficulties, even if you are usually reliable, you reduce the perception of your indispensability. Each deadline you miss, each problem that stymies you, gives your bosses feelings they do not want to have and you do not want them to have. Sooner or later, they will begin thinking about shedding the source of their unpleasant feelings.

If you miss a deadline, provide an explanation, not an excuse. The explanation should include both a promise that the inadequate performance will not be repeated and a plan for how you intend to avoid such a repetition. Then move heaven and earth to keep your promise and adhere to your plan. If it means working late, work late. If it means calling in favors from colleagues, call them in. Establishing a clutch brand requires a "mission-critical" level of commitment at all times. As hard as you may be on yourself, your bosses can always be harder.

4. Be the Customer-Satisfaction Brand

Work as if your life depended on every customer you serve. Professionally speaking, this is not hyperbole. Your professional life does for a fact depend on each of your customers, especially when the national rate of unemployment hovers around one in every ten workers.

Customers come in two varieties. There are external customers, who include clients you may work with or consumers to whom you sell actual merchandise. And there are internal customers, who are the subordinates, colleagues, and bosses with whom you work every day. Like external customers, internal customers expect you to deliver value and satisfaction to them—not just some of the time, but all of the time.

Satisfy Current Customers While Winning New Customers

Sell to every customer you can, whether that means persuading an office manager to purchase your firm's accounting software or persuading your boss that your work is of the highest value. Satisfy your current customers while making new ones. Where internal customers are concerned, endeavor to extend your influence by serving an expanding range of colleagues and managers in your department and beyond. Growing your internal customer base will heighten your visibility within the organization and add to your professional network. Both of these outcomes improve your chances for advancement (in the best case) or holding on to what you've got (in the worst).

Resolve to keep your external and internal customers happy by providing the best possible service and the highest value. Branding yourself as a creator of customer satisfaction will increase both your perceived and actual value to the organization.

Follow-Up Behavior

Satisfying customers goes beyond the original sale. Follow-up is key. Ensure that you respond to phone calls and emails promptly and fully. When a customer asks a question or presents you with a problem, take ownership of it. This means that you cannot let go of the question without answering it or the problem without solving it—or finding someone who can answer the question or solve the problem. Under no circumstances do you have license to abandon the customer. If your internal as well as external customers consistently come to you, rely on you, and seek you, it is far less likely that, even in hard times, you will find yourself pushed out the door. If customers want you, you are, by definition, indispensable.

Ask Questions

Answering questions and solving problems is never a monologue. Ask the customer questions. Find out exactly what he needs and what he wants. Questions are not a sign of ignorance; they are a mark of intelligence. It makes no sense to guess at a client's needs when you can simply ask.

And don't confine your questions to the customer. When an internal or external customer raises an issue for which you do not have a ready response, find someone who can supply the necessary information: "Tom, I'm not familiar with that version of the software upgrade, but I know just the person to ask about it. May I put you on hold, so that I can get Marie Williams on the line? She will be able to help us out."

There is no virtue in speaking or acting from a lack of knowledge when appropriate sources of knowledge are available to you. When a customer asks a question or asks you to do something, it is obviously best to deliver the right response or to do the correct thing the first time. Errors not only look bad, they decrease confidence, consume time, and erode customer satisfaction. Besides, asking questions demonstrates to others in your organization your commitment to your customer and your desire to be fully involved in processes vital to the enterprise.

Extra Mile Service

Decide right now that your customers—all of them, internal and external—are worth going that extra mile to serve. In an age of email and smartphones, being physically absent from the office is no excuse for failing to serve a customer. If you are out of the office, even if you are on vacation, take as many customer calls as you can. Better yet, when you need to be out of the office for any extended period of time, make certain that your customers are covered by a buddy or other designated pinch hitter. If your customer still calls you, don't just send her to the pinch hitter. Make the connection for her, if possible via conference call: "Christine, I'm out of the office, but Sam Johnson is on top of your business with us and will take care of you. May I place you on hold for a moment while I get him on the line?"

"You're Right, But . . ."

The old saw about the customer always being right is not, of course, literally true. Your job is to guide and advise your customers. After all, knowingly selling someone the wrong thing—whether it's a machine part or an internal document you know they don't need—will not create satisfaction. On the other hand, you must resist the temptation to demonstrate your superior knowledge. Consider the following exchange:

> **Customer:** What I want is the 250-watt model. I need the power.
> **You:** Well, you may want it, but you can't have it. You'll blow out the panel. I'll sell you the 150. That's what you need.

Of course, it is your responsibility to protect the customer from doing something stupid. But it is also your responsibility to satisfy him by giving him what he wants. The problem with the response above is that it targets the customer's error but ignores what the customer says he wants: "the power." Here is a better response:

> **Customer:** What I want is the 250-watt model. I need the power.
> **You:** Bill, the panel you have is rated at 150 and would be overloaded by the 250-watt model. If you really do need the extra power—and I can understand why you would want it—then we will have to upgrade your panel. I can give you a price on this, if you like.

Even when a customer is mistaken, look for ways to say "you're right" or "you're right, but." Nothing is to be gained by making a customer feel stupid or thwarted. You don't want him to hang up the phone with the memory of his mistake and your correction, but with the feeling that he asked for something and you figured out a way to give it to him.

Smile

Before the days of self-service gas stations, oil companies used to advertise "Service with a Smile." The old-fashioned corner "filling station" may have vanished, but the idea of delivering customer service pleasantly, cheerfully, and with enthusiasm—as if you regarded serving the customer as a privilege rather than a burden—will never go out of style.

5. Be the Feel-Good Brand

Carry that idea of "Service with a Smile" into everything you do. The familiar expression about the squeaky wheel getting the grease will not serve you well in the workplace. If you're whining, stop it. Nobody likes a complainer, especially in the context of a collaborative endeavor. Whining is egocentric. The myriad injustices you may feel have been inflicted on you will never become a popular cause. Instead of whining, be a team player who focuses on making things better for the firm, the department, and the team, and things will be better for you, too.

Bottle It Up

Daytime TV psycho-gurus tells us never to bottle up our feelings, no matter how unpleasant. Well, unless you want to be handed a whole lot more time to watch television in the afternoon, chuck their advice and start bottling. Try to avoid making a single negative observation. Don't express a single complaint—not about your boss, not about the annoying hum of the fluorescent lights, not about the solid gloomy week of rainy weather. Keep your nose down and work. Be busy, and look busy.

If you are worried about the economy in general or the future of the company in particular, put on an optimistic act. During World War II, the hard scowl of General George S. Patton Jr. became as much of a trademark as the ivory-handled six-shooter he strapped to his belt. But that scowl didn't come naturally to Patton. He called it his "war face," and he practiced it in front of a mirror every chance he got.

In today's workplace, your "war face" is a smile, and if it doesn't come naturally to you—or you just don't feel like smiling much these days—take a leaf from the book of Patton. Practice putting on your work mask before you leave home in the morning. Wear that mask religiously. Smile, and no one will ask you "What's wrong?" You may still *feel* that plenty is wrong, but once people actually start asking you that question, you might as well head for the nearest exit, because you are on your way out.

Speaking of exits, don't ever walk through your boss's "open-door policy," no matter how genial and sincere the invitation. With the best intentions, your boss may invite you and everyone else to tell him about problems: "My door is always open." He may even solicit: "How's it going?" or "What's wrong?" Never walk through the boss's open door to complain.

There Is No Refuge

Don't think you can take refuge in the quality of your work. If you think nobody will mind your whining as long as you maintain a high level of competent productivity, understand that human resources research has consistently shown that most people would rather work with a marginally incompetent but always friendly colleague than a super-capable whiner. They understand that negativity is contagious and can soon infect an entire office. On the flip side, your can-do, smiling presence will also permeate your work group, encouraging others to take a positive approach to their work, and, in tough times, a positive approach is more important than ever. Not only will management want to keep you around, business may measurably improve.

6. Be the Popular Brand

That smile you're working on sends a powerful, primal signal to others. It is welcoming instead of off-putting. It invites others to deal with you, to work with you, to accept you and your ideas. Your smile—your "work mask," if that is what it must be—is one tool in a toolbox intended to prevent workplace isolation.

Being recognized as a member of the workplace community strengthens your position in the organization. Isolation weakens it. This is not rocket science, but common sense. If you are not perceived as part of the community, no one will feel much regret over showing you the door.

Chapter 5 was devoted to creating "uncommon courtesy" in the workplace. The reason for making that effort is to prevent job-killing, career-killing isolation. Greet the people you work with. Show interest in them and their lives. Talk, listen—especially listen—and you will likely find the people you work with are very interesting.

You have a life outside of work, and integrating yourself into the workplace community does not require that you abandon your family so that you can hang out with the gang each and every evening after quitting time. But don't make refusing invites to have a beer your knee-jerk response. Never give the impression that you are unfriendly or that you are too good to mix with the people you work with.

Steer Clear of Egomania

Contrary to received workaday wisdom, having a strong sense of self—a solid ego—is a quality that commands respect and admiration. What nobody likes, however, is an egomaniac, a person interested only in himself, whose only topic of conversation is himself, and whose only tune is the sound of his own horn tooting. Not only are such people obnoxious and dull, they are by definition lacking in value to a collaborative business enterprise. Expressing concern only for themselves, they seem to be saying that they have no room in their minds or hearts for the rest of the company—the company on which *your* welfare depends.

The surest way to avoid falling into the trap of egomania is to make sure that your conversation with coworkers, subordinates, and bosses consists of a lot more questions than declarative statements. As long as you are asking somebody something about what that person feels, thinks, or is doing, you are demonstrating that your sphere of concern extends far beyond yourself.

Give, Don't Take, Credit

Some egomaniacs are just boring and obnoxious, and that's bad enough. Others, however, make themselves downright dangerous. These are the people who do not scruple to take credit for the ideas, the comments, the judgments, or the work of others. If you find yourself guilty of this on occasion, now is the time to repent and reform. In the first place, people will soon hate you for this behavior. Before long, you may find a knife or two or more protruding from your back. In the second place, the practice is so fundamentally dishonest that, sooner or later, it will percolate up to management, where it could be the basis for dismissal.

Instead of trying to claim credit, give credit—and do so generously. When anyone you work with achieves something of value, has a good idea, passes a milestone, be the cheerleader who celebrates the accomplishment. Not only will the recipient of the acknowledgment, praise, or congratulations feel good about herself—and therefore feel good about you—everyone will admire your generosity of spirit and your teamsmanship.

Networks and Mentors

Too many of us think of networking as establishing professional connections strictly outside of our current workplace. While it is important to network in this way, it is at least equally essential to network within your current place of employment. Not only will this plug you into opportunities in other areas of the company, it will integrate you more fully within the workplace community. The more connections you make, the more visible you become, and the more visible you are, the less easy it will be for management to add you to the expendable list.

As for mentoring, you don't have to limit yourself to identifying and attaching yourself to a formal mentor. Make an effort to learn, informally and as the opportunities present themselves, from the most experienced and respected people in the office. Doing so will not only establish connections between you and them, it will give you many opportunities to hone your skills and boost your productivity. From such informal relationships, more extensive mentor relationships may develop.

Build Respect

It is important that the people with whom you work like you, but you should be building toward something beyond mere affection. You want the workplace community to *respect* you and your abilities. If you are respected, others will seek you out for your advice and, yes, even your mentoring. Their demonstrations of respect will cement your place within the community. You will be recognized as a sought-after resource, and everyone, management included, will want you to stick around.

7. Be the Loyal and Dedicated Brand

The language of business may be money, but, in the end, money isn't everything. Everyone has to make a living, and no one expects you to work for free, but avoid broadcasting the impression that you are working first and last for a paycheck—even if that is precisely what you are doing. It is to your advantage that others believe your work means more to you than punching a clock.

1. Work as long as you must to get the job done, even if this means staying behind after others have left. Be task oriented, not time defined.

2. Offer help and lots of it.

3. When your offer of help is accepted, take ownership of whatever problems you are working on. They are yours until they are solved.

4. Take on more work. Volunteer.

Cultivate an image of dedication and loyalty, and you will transform your image from that of an expendable commodity into that of a human being who wants to make a genuine contribution to the enterprise.

8. Be the High-Value Brand

Savvy consumers don't shop for *price*, they shop for *value*—bang for the buck. Savvy employers look at their human capital in much the same way, in terms of return on investment. To be perceived as the high-value brand, take every opportunity possible to show value. If you are not clearly adding value to your employer, she's going to find it increasingly difficult to justify keeping you around. Your employer is trading value—the price of a paycheck—for the value you provide. She will not long tolerate an imbalance of value unfavorable to her.

Review Chapters 2 through 4 for ways to identify and present your value. In addition, roll up your sleeves and do the following:

- **Show that you are hungry.** Crave more work. Volunteer. If you've finished all of your projects, ask your boss for more or, better yet, take the initiative by inventing more (genuinely productive) work for yourself.

- **Focus on doing what you can do well.** Be hungry, but don't be a slob. Pile your plate high, but choose the right projects. Doing a lot of work is important. Doing a lot of work badly is disastrous. Superb execution is more important than sheer volume.

- **Increase your productivity measurably.** This will mean working harder—probably longer hours—but also working smarter, becoming more efficient so that you produce more in a shorter span of time.

- **Show up on time every day.** In fact, show up ten or fifteen minutes early.

- **Brand yourself as a workhorse.** The newer you are to the firm, the more important this is.

- **Immerse yourself in your business.** Learn everything you can about it. Get cozy with your suppliers and your customers. Understand what the competition is doing. Apply your knowledge to your job, while also offering yourself as a valuable source of information throughout your department, work group, and company. ("We can't lose Joe. He's the guy who knows everything.")

- **Keep a pad and paper handy.** Take notes when the boss or other senior employees speak. Demonstrate that you are learning on the job.

9. Be the High-Sales Brand

Sell, sell, then sell some more.

Promote your company when you're on the outside. At conventions, at cocktail parties, at Little League games with other parents, playing golf or tennis, sell the value of your firm. Within the company, sell the value of your department: "John, we take every opportunity we can in Customer Service to steer folks back to you guys in Sales. We're big believers in up-selling." Make yourself a dedicated advocate for the source of your income.

And don't just promote the firm. Promote yourself at all times as well. Document your achievements and pass the information on up. Ask your satisfied clients and customers to express their satisfaction to your boss. (Just make sure you *have* satisfied them.) Be your own advocate and champion. Let the numbers do your boasting. Track measurable results. Share those results with the people who have the power to advance and reward you.

10. Be the Bottom-Line Brand

The bottom line should always be in your thoughts, but never more than when the economy is soft. In these periods, nickels and dimes matter, and management starts counting them. This is the time to really start looking for ways to contribute directly to the bottom line. Not only can cost savings save your job—by leaving enough money at the end of each month to pay you—your efforts also demonstrate your "selfless" commitment to the well-being of the enterprise. Employers want value for the value they invest. This may be measured in the value you generate as well as in the value you save.

Look for Deals

Actively look for ways to bolster the bottom line. Is some item of new technology the answer? Research it. Should the company partner with the local community college or high school to start a low-cost internship program? Does Vendor A offer a better deal than Vendor B on printer ink? Can a routine procedure be streamlined?

Mine New Sources of Revenue

The real gold, as far as you are concerned, may be found in discovering new revenue streams that require little or no investment. For example, some routine customer service functions might be revamped as opportunities for sales:

> **Customer service rep to customer who has called for a repair:** Mr. Smith, you might consider investing in a new widget module, which has a duty cycle of 10,000 hours instead of the 5,000-hour model you're using now. I know most customers think of this as heavy duty, so they settle for the 5,000-hour model, which is certainly less expensive, but when you factor in the cost of the service call and the downtime, you may decide the extra up-front cash is well worth it.

Do More with Less

Practice creative austerity by devising ways to do more with less. Share your ideas with the boss and others who have the power to advance you. A few years ago, the phrase "guerilla marketing" emerged to describe the practice of identifying cheap or free channels for reaching your customers. Stretch your company's marketing and advertising dollars by identifying and formulating creative ways to use social media (Twitter, Spoke, Facebook, LinkedIn, YouTube, and the like) and other forms of free but effective publicity. Promote these with your boss as a means of leveraging your existing paid advertising programs.

11. Be the All-Purpose Brand

Review Chapters 2 through 4 to help you compose a menu of all that you bring to your employer's table. Identify the things you do that measurably help the company. Look at that menu and decide which of those things are also uniquely yours—your specialties. These constitute the core of your brand. Play them up. Build on them. Promote them. And grow out from them. Expand your menu.

Get Uncomfortable

Be willing to step outside your comfort zone and push out the boundaries of your job description. If you can do more than you do now, you may save your employer the need to hire another worker. You don't want to transform yourself from a highly skilled specialist into a jack-of-all-trades and master of none, but every team needs a utility player, someone who can go beyond the expected. Layoffs and downsizing have magnified the value of such players. Now, therefore, is a great time to step into the utility role.

Learn

Expand your areas of expertise. Multiply your qualifications. Make your job as big as it can be. Be sure your bosses recognize just how big your job has become.

If your company offers learning programs, investigate them and take full advantage of those that most interest you and that are most likely to help you develop your position. Remember, many companies offer tuition assistance for night classes and other programs.

Demonstrate Flexibility

Show a willingness to move into new positions and even to retrain. Your commitment should be to your firm, not to the position you happen to occupy. This is where the concept of transferable skills, discussed in Part One of this book, comes into play.

If necessary, reinvent yourself. Shifts in technology and markets may combine with a softening economy to endanger some positions while making others more attractive. Leverage your experience and your transferable skill set to reinvent yourself so that you may shed liabilities and embrace new opportunities. If you are an administrator, consider boosting your tech skills. If you are already a techie, broaden out into administration.

12. Defend Your Brands

The eleven exercises in branding I've just outlined are all meant as proactive steps that will position you to advance, even in adverse times. Your brands are valuable and worth protecting. Here's some guidance on how to defend them.

Pull in Your Horns

We Americans love our freedom of speech. Maybe, however, the time has come to watch what you say. Least offensive is always most desirable. Keep your political and religious opinions to yourself.

This advice goes for national affairs as well as company business. Try to appear politically neutral across the board. Don't ally yourself with any particular faction at work. If you connect too closely with your boss, he will drag you down if he gets fired. Cooperate, collaborate, be helpful, and act at all times like a team player, but never forget that your deepest loyalty is first and foremost to yourself.

Leave Gossip to the Tabloids

Gossip- and rumor-mongering are features of working life. Nevertheless, avoid idle chatter—which makes you look like a goof-off—and refuse to be either the source or the vessel of gossip. The tales you tell or convey have an ugly habit of coming back to bite you.

Emails Are Strictly Business

The emails you send using a company computer on a company network are the property of the company. You do not control them. You cannot decide who reads them. You cannot dictate how they are used or not used. For these reasons, never send personal emails using company equipment. Regardless of the identity of your intended recipient, write nothing that you would not want your boss to read.

Emails can be deleted, but deleting them does not obliterate them. Most enterprise networks save emails in a master file. For better or worse, your words are deathless and available to management.

Office Romance

Many human resources professionals warn against office romances. Some even declare them to be career killers. But the real-world truth is that most people meet their significant others at work. There is nothing mysterious about this, since work is where you spend at least half of your waking life.

If it is unrealistic to demand total abstinence from office romance, it is still important to face certain realities concerning it:

- Ask yourself whether the attraction is based on mutual affection or on perceived career gain.

- If you are a manager or in any way senior to the other person, ask yourself whether he or she would say yes if you weren't in a position of power.

- Before you embark on an office romance, know your company's policy on the subject. Most midsize and larger corporations have explicit policies forbidding sexual harassment, but only about 6 percent of companies have written policies on mutually consenting "fraternization." Of this 6 percent, almost none ban office romance between single, consenting adults—though about a third of companies have stated policies that define public displays of affection as inappropriate.

- Policy or not, be discreet. No one benefits from the display of dating behavior in the workplace.

- Be assured of this: If you go out on more than a couple of dates, the entire office *will* discover your "secret." The two partners in a relationship should agree on whom they will tell and what they will say.

- It should go without saying that an office romance is only an office *romance* if it takes place between two fully consenting adults. Anything other than this is not romance, but sexual harassment, which is not only a potential career killer, but also cause for civil and possibly even criminal action.

Take a Salary Cut Gracefully

The "unkindest cut of all," to paraphrase Shakespeare, is being cut from the rolls of the employed. Coming in second—albeit a *distant* second—is being offered the choice between taking a salary cut or losing your job.

It is, of course, not much of a choice—at least not in a down economy and tight employment market in which jobs are few and far between. But it does leave you with plenty of choice about how you accept the "deal." You can be bitter and make your boss feel bad or angry or both, or you can demonstrate your commitment to the firm by smiling and saying, "I know it's all for the good of the company. I'll do with less for now."

Having taken a bullet for the company while waving the company flag to boot, don't be in too big a hurry to swallow hook, line, and sinker your own smiling reply to your boss. By all means, consider yourself lucky to have a job—if only because it is much easier to apply for another job from a position of employment. But while holding on, do not give up on the goal of continuing to advance. Take less now, but start looking for more.

CHAPTER 8

CREATING SATISFACTION

Nothing makes you more indispensable at work than consistently creating satisfaction. Everyone knows how important it is to satisfy customers, but few of us understand that we always have *two* sets of customers to satisfy. There are, of course, your "external" customers—the people with whom you and your firm do business, the people on the other side of your counter. But there are also your "internal" customers. These include colleagues, people who report to you, and the people to whom you report: your boss or bosses.

All of your internal customers are important, but none, naturally, is more important than your boss.

Never forget that your boss is a customer: somebody who trades value (a paycheck) in the expectation of receiving value (your productivity). To deliver total satisfaction to this key customer, you need to make it your business to know as much about his needs, wants, and expectations as you possibly can. That is the focus of this chapter.

The Eternal Truth, Part 1

Through all changes in economic reality, the marketplace, technology, and management styles, one truth remains eternal: However you present yourself, however much you are liked, there is no substitute for knowing your job and doing your job well. If you consistently produce an unsatisfactory work product, you will fail to create satisfaction in your customer, and you will lose your job.

The Eternal Truth, Part 2

While Part 1 is eternally true, there is also a Part 2, equally changeless in its validity: Being well liked may allow you to hold on to your job far longer than your by-the-numbers performance merits.

As mentioned in Chapter 6, many people, including bosses, express a preference for working with likable colleagues even if they are less than 100 percent competent. At best, however, in the absence of satisfactory performance, getting the boss to like you will postpone rather than prevent your termination. On the other hand—and this is the most significant aspect of Part 2 of the Eternal Truth—being a top performer does not guarantee that you will hang on to your job, let alone achieve advancement.

Doubtless your parents warned you that life isn't always fair. Well, this is what they meant. Perform at 100 percent, and you should be rewarded. And maybe you *will* be rewarded. But maybe not.

Your task is not to lament that "maybe not," but to do something positive to minimize it. To satisfy your boss-customer, endeavor to deliver nothing but top-quality work *and* to create in her all the right feelings about you and what you do. Be guided by the requirements of both parts of the Eternal

Truth, and your odds of not only keeping your job but of growing in it and even beyond it will increase significantly. Satisfy your customer and you will build the brand that is you, making that brand indispensable.

You Set the Tone

Parents, teachers, Dutch uncles, and others who shape our childhoods tell us "You can't please everybody" and "You can't make everyone like you." These statements not only fall into the *so-trite-they're-true* category, they must also be slid onto the *half-truth* shelf. While you cannot please everybody and you cannot make everyone like you, you should nevertheless persist in setting these impossibilities as the twin goals toward which you shape your behavior. True, you cannot control what others feel and do, but you can influence the set of feelings that produce the actions you want from other people. And while you cannot directly control your boss's feelings—about you or about anything else—you can do a great deal to set the tone of the relationship and thereby steer her feelings in your favor.

Put on a Really Good Act

This brings us to yet another trite-but-true observation: You can't make others feel good about you if you don't feel good about yourself.

It would be foolish to deny that self-confidence is a really useful asset to possess, but don't be downhearted if you are a little shy or even an outright self-doubter. No need to put off a conversation with your boss until you've got a dozen years of intensive psychotherapy under your belt. No one can read your mind or peer into the depths of your heart. All they can do is read your actions and your words.

So begin with your actions.

Set the Tone Without Saying a Word

Body language is a powerful communicator, and like anything powerful, it can do a great deal of good or a great deal of harm, depending on how you use or fail to use it.

Start with how you breathe. Breathing is a natural process, naturally, but you *can* learn to make it work for you, not against you. When you are excited or frightened, you breathe more rapidly and less deeply. The result is that you look scared, and you sound scared. When you are anxious, you speak in the voice of fear, a tone that is thin, tight, quavering, high-pitched, and utterly unpersuasive. It is the tone many of us unconsciously adopt when we speak to an authority figure—a teacher, a police officer, a boss. Now, you may not be able to suppress the anxiety. Trying to tamp down or deny feelings is a lot like dieting. *Try* to diet, and you often end up thinking about nothing but food, which makes you hungrier than ever. *Try* to deny a feeling, and that feeling becomes uppermost in your mind. Instead of focusing on what you *feel*, therefore, let your feelings fend for themselves while you work on regulating how you *act*.

- Breathe more productively. When you are anxious and therefore breathing rapidly, your natural inclination is to try to calm yourself down by taking a few deep breaths. Contrary to instinct, this is not the most effective way to stop hyperventilating (the rapid, shallow breathing associated with anxiety). Instead of taking a few deep breaths, try (in the privacy of your office or even the restroom) panting rapidly, concentrating more on exhaling than inhaling. This will raise the level of carbon dioxide in your blood, which will automatically slow your breathing to a more relaxed rate.

- Once you have your breathing under more productive control, pay attention to your voice. People find a deep voice more persuasive—

more authoritative—than a higher-pitched voice. This is true whether you are a man or a woman. While a soprano cannot transform herself into a bass (and, believe me, the result would not be pretty, even if it were achievable), anyone can practice using the lower register of the voice they have. Consciously lower the pitch of your voice. Practice doing so. Get into the habit of making this lower pitch the register of your public voice.

- When you lower your voice, you will probably find that you also slow down the pace of your conversation and enunciate more carefully. Good. While speaking very slowly is not an effective tactic for persuasion, speaking at a pace that gives each word weight and meaning makes you sound intelligent and articulate, thereby endowing what you have to say with greater perceived value. By way of bonus, speaking a bit more slowly than normal will also help to ensure that you do not become short of breath. Bear in mind that fast talking has a negative connotation in our culture, especially our business culture. There is a good reason why "fast talker" is a synonym for a swindler, a glib character who tries to put one over on those he deals with. At the very least, talking too fast tells the other person that you are uncomfortable and want to make your getaway. Relax, lower your voice, and slow down.

Act Your Age

For many of us, it is not just anxiety that kicks in when we deal with the boss, it is a scenario out of childhood. Because the boss is an authority figure, we unconsciously respond to him as a child to a parent. This often comes across nonverbally, through body language. Watch out for the following childish behaviors:

- **Failure to make and maintain eye contact.** Children have trouble looking the adult authority figure in the eye. Consciously make and maintain eye contact. This doesn't mean trying to stare down your boss (the "stare down" is childish behavior of another kind), but when you speak and when you listen, it is important to look him in the eye, one adult to another.

- **Fidgeting and squirming.** By all means, gesture when speaking. Look alive and lively. Just make sure your movements are purposeful and help to convey your meaning.

- **Covering your mouth or putting your fingers to your mouth area, especially when speaking.** An adult talking to another adult keeps her hands away from her face.

- **Hands in pockets.** An unmistakable throwback to childhood, especially for men. This also looks like you have something to hide. Keep your hands out and visible when you speak. Use open gestures, palms up. This suggests both honesty and openness to what the other person has to say.

The beauty of *acting* your age is that you don't have to *feel* your age. If talking to your boss makes you feel like a little girl or boy, don't deny the feeling. Just don't act on it. Practice adult gestures, and you will not only be perceived as an adult, but begin to feel more and more like one, regardless of the identity or status of your partner in conversation.

Practice Good Timing

Strive to get in synch with the rhythms and routines of your workplace. This is key to giving your boss the message that you fit in and are a team player.

Observe your boss. What's her daily routine? Are there good and not-so-good times to have a conversation? Discover these, then try to exploit the good times while avoiding the bad.

Every workplace is different, of course, but some principles of timing are more or less universal:

- Unless an issue is pressing or an opportunity may be lost, avoid conversations on Monday that can be conducted on Tuesday.

- Avoid raising important, complex, or disturbing issues immediately before lunch or at the very end of the day. Also avoid bringing them up just before a weekend or immediately before either you or your boss is taking time off. Don't bring up an action item if you will not be present to take action on it, and don't give your boss something to stew about on the beach.

- If your boss doesn't really want to talk, don't push him. "I haven't got much time" or "I'm off to a meeting" or "I've just got a minute" are all ways of saying "I don't want to talk right now." Unless the issue is genuinely urgent *to the organization*, hold off. Return at a more opportune time.

Make an Offer

Most conversations with the boss are for the purpose either of reporting something or of asking for something. That it should be so makes perfect sense. Nine times out of ten, either bosses want information from you or you want to get something from them. Nevertheless, try approaching your next conversation not as an occasion simply to report or as an occasion simply to ask, but instead as an opportunity to offer.

Don't approach a conversation with the boss as a passive delivery of data on the one hand or as a supplication on the other, a request for something in return for nothing. Instead, treat every encounter as a negotiation, a pledge to return value for value received.

Consistently offer value in what you say, and your boss will not only welcome the words you bring her, but will come to think of you as her go-to brand: absolutely indispensable. Here is the communication strategy for making this transition happen:

- It is hard to feel very persuasive when you have your hand out. Walking into your boss's office with something to offer gives you greater confidence in your own case; therefore, prepare your offering beforehand. Spontaneity is overrated. Face time with your boss is too valuable to squander on improvisation. Plan what you have to say. You should consider making a written outline; don't bring it with you, but do review it before your appointment. You may even find it helpful to rehearse—or at least to try out your end of the conversation on a friend.

- Like a good salesman, focus on what your customer wants, not on your needs. By satisfying the customer, you will take care of your needs.

- Prepare for conversations with your boss by asking yourself what it is he needs and wants. What really good news can you bring him? What issues of concern to your boss can you raise? What problems that concern your boss can you offer to solve?

Exercise Empathy

To get into your boss's head, walk a mile in his shoes. Empathize. To satisfy this customer, see the world from her point of view. But take care not to confuse *empathy* with *sympathy*. Empathy has nothing to do with feeling sorry for someone. It is the ability to put yourself in another's place, to see reality from his or her point of view. If you want to understand your customer, so that you can sell to her more effectively, you empathize—you endeavor to see reality from her point of view. If you want to understand your boss, so that you can sell your value to him more effectively, you need to exercise the same degree of empathy.

The most effective way to empathize with your boss is to learn about the nature of leadership. Not only will this prepare you for dealing more effectively with your boss, it will also prepare you for entering a leadership role at some point in your career. While learning all about your customer/boss, you'll be preparing yourself to rise to the next level in your career.

Start with People You Admire

Want to learn about being the boss? Talk to your boss, and talk to other leaders you work with and admire. Actually converse with them about what it means to be a leader. Understand that, job titles notwithstanding, not every boss is a leader. Vast libraries have been written about the "secrets of leadership," but there is a valid *short* answer to the question *What makes a leader?* It is this: The values and traits most of us admire in businesspeople are the values and traits of a leader. Therefore, think about the businesspeople you most admire. Now ask yourself what it is that makes you admire them.

Everyone will answer this question with a different list, but, without a doubt, there will be at least one universal element: *credibility*. It is the universal quality that makes one worthy of leadership.

Three elements are essential to the possession of leadership-grade credibility:

- **Leaders know what they know and what they don't know.** You will discover that leaders are typically self-confident and sure of themselves. Some people are lucky enough to be born that way, but you don't have to be. Confidence and self-assurance come from knowing your job, knowing your facts, knowing the basis for your own decisions and opinions, and—just as important as all this—knowing what you *don't* know: understanding the limits of your knowledge.

- **Leaders listen.** Leadership credibility has more to do with listening intelligently and productively than with speaking. Effective leaders listen, learn, and respond with words that address the issues they have heard.

- **Leaders are not defensive.** They express themselves with self-assurance, then invite response, including frank criticism. An effective leader never attempts to shout down her critics. She learns from them and invites multiple points of view.

Understand leadership credibility in this way, and you will find yourself able to deal more effectively with your bosses, especially the best of them.

Boss Imperfect

Unfortunately, not all bosses are "the best of them." Most, in fact, operate somewhere along a spectrum bounded at either end by "best" and "worst."

You should begin by assuming the best—that is, by giving your boss the benefit of the doubt and taking for granted that he merits credibility for his knowledge of what he knows and does not know, his willingness to listen, and his openness to ideas and criticism. Adjust these assumptions as you acquire more experience working with your boss. Identifying your boss's deficiencies and sore spots is essential to building a bond of mutual loyalty with him and thereby transforming him into a thoroughly satisfied customer. The imperfections of most bosses fall under one or more of four categories:

1. My Way or the Highway

Some leaders tend toward a narrowly authoritarian approach that affords little or no latitude for the ideas of others and that is generally intolerant of criticism. These bosses see themselves as absolute authorities. The style that goes along with this attitude includes difficulty having discussion, since, for the authoritarian boss, monologue is always preferable to dialogue. On the rare occasions when the authoritarian boss does ask questions, it is less to gather information than to "keep you on your toes." The authoritarian boss does not solicit answers, he demands them, and he does not scruple at making threats, which are often couched in sentences that begin with "You'd better," which always implies an "or else."

You will find that authoritarian bosses shun spontaneity and improvisation. They tend to be rigid, often responding to your requests by quoting company rules and company policy. Understand that the authoritarian boss sees the corporate hierarchy or chain of command in rigid terms. If your boss is at the mid level, how hard he comes down on you is directly proportionate to his perception of how hard his boss or bosses come down on him. The authoritarian boss tends to be reactive rather than proactive.

Depending on your own personality, you may find dealing with an authoritarian manager nearly intolerable or gratifyingly straightforward (because you always know where you stand). If you find it difficult to get along with this type of manager, your best approach is to begin by putting the boss in perspective. What, exactly, can he actually do to you? Does he have the power to fire you? And, if he does, has he fired a lot of other people before? Chances are that much of the authoritarian style is just that, *style*. Assess the bark versus the bite, then devise ways to satisfy *this* customer. For instance:

- Make him feel good about something, anything—from his choice of necktie to a recent management decision.

- Follow orders efficiently and to the letter. Minimize improvisation.

- Ask for advice. This is always an empowering request—and the more power an authoritarian boss believes he is acquiring, the better he will feel about himself, and the better he will treat you.

If your boss criticizes you, accept the criticism with gratitude:

Boss: I'm disappointed in you. Turnaround times have hardly improved.
You: I'm disappointed, too. I expected more progress at this point, and I was about to come to you for your advice on the present situation. When can we get together and discuss a strategic approach to improving turnaround?

2. Finger Pointers

Some bosses are "picky"—hypercritical—and some simply seem incapable of controlling their need to point accusatory fingers and deal out blame. Before you label your boss as a blamer, objectively assess the situation. Part of a manager's legitimate job is to criticize results in order to improve performance. Begin by assuming that your boss's criticism is not only justified, but helpful, before you conclude that she's just out to get you.

Once you conclude, as objectively as possible, that you are being blamed for something that is not your fault, don't be too quick to defend yourself. Instead, without accepting *blame*, accept *responsibility* by offering to pitch in to correct the problem—even though you did not cause it. Before responding to any accusation or criticism, make sure that you:

- Get all the facts. Resist the temptation to spew out a stream of denials. Instead, reply that you will research the situation, get the facts, and work to make everything right. It is always best to shift the focus from emotions and personalities to causes, effects, facts, and the promise of satisfactory results.

- Confront the event rather than the accusation. Don't argue with angry words. Listen. Then deal with the situation, not the personality of the boss.

- If you are unjustly blamed, accept responsibility, but not the blame: "I understand that the customer is unhappy; however, I did not make the promises he has told you about. Nevertheless, he *is* my customer, and I own the problem. I will resolve this to his satisfaction and yours."

- Respond with a promise of cooperation rather than denial, contradiction, or challenge to your boss.

3. The Bumbler

Followers often make a sport of questioning the competence of their leaders. Judge results rather than personality. Does your boss routinely forget appointments, lose track of details, habitually thrash around instead of making necessary decisions, or fail to meet production and revenue targets? If so, he may be marginally incompetent or even worse. Your best moves in dealing with this kind of boss include:

- Being patient. Do not express exasperation.

- Resisting the urge to complain about your boss to others.

- Dotting your i's and crossing your t's. Confirm instructions and correct errors. Avoid a mocking or patronizing tone.

- Putting everything in writing. Confirm verbal instructions by email or even by paper memo.

- Being as helpful as possible. Provide guidance.

4. The Volatile Boss

Some bosses explode—and even take pride in being known as screamers ("I'm passionate about what I do!"). Such behavior is incompatible with the best management. An explosive personality discourages communication, and while some people may be intimidated by screaming, intimidation and fear do not usually motivate top-level performance. Instead, they tend to motivate avoidance of confrontation and conflict. Sometimes they motivate a search for a new job and a new boss.

Your number one imperative in dealing with a volatile boss is to master your own fear reaction. Here are ways to cope:

- When the emotional volcano erupts, let the lava flow harmlessly around you. Endure the tirade. If you are being lectured to or even yelled at, maintain a calm expression and do not break eye contact. On your side, try to act as if you are having a routine conversation.

- Look for an opportunity to defuse the situation. When you can get a word in edgewise, acknowledge the anger: "I can't blame you, for being angry, but . . ." Then introduce alternatives to the tirade: "but I need to talk this through with you to arrive at a solution to the problem."

- Empower your boss by providing alternatives: "Do you want to sit down and discuss this now, or should I come back?"

- Analyze the issues. Address them. You will find that performance is the most effective antidote to an angry outburst.

The Ties That Bind

Even highly imperfect bosses are human beings with whom you can create a loyalty bond that makes your working life not only easier, but more secure. It is not always easy to recognize where bonding leaves off and out-and-out sucking up begins. Two-way loyalty between you and your boss is built on an efficient and productive working relationship between two adults, not between a parent and child and certainly not between a master and servant. It's mostly about saying the right things at the right times.

Learn to Take a Compliment

If it feels good to get a compliment from your boss, your boss also feels good in giving it—provided that you accept the compliment with grace and generosity.

Your boss praises you for two reasons: First, to give you good feelings about your work and about your relationship with her. Second, to reinforce the behavior that occasioned the compliment so that it will be repeated. Both of these motives present you with a golden opportunity to bond with your boss. Seize the opportunity and make the most of it.

You may consider yourself "one of those people" who isn't "good with compliments." Okay, fine. But understand that accepting a compliment gracefully is not a matter of personal preference, it's business, it's part of your job. Put aside modesty and do the following:

- Smile broadly.

- Say "Thank you" while smiling broadly.

- Respond with a compliment to the giver of the compliment: "Coming from you, that really means something." Make the most of this opportunity to express your high regard for your boss.

- Share the praise with others who deserve it, giving credit to colleagues and coworkers involved in the project or on the team. "I couldn't have done this without my team."

In addition to "Thank you," try to use the following:

"I am grateful for the opportunity."
"I had a great team."
"I look forward to the next challenge."
"It's a win for all of us."
"That's great to hear."
"Your support made this possible."
"Your support meant a lot in this."

Just as important as saying the right thing is not saying the wrong. Never confess your unworthiness to accept the compliment ("I really don't deserve this"), and don't deliver a long speech in response. Avoid anything that resembles the following:

"I almost didn't make it."
"I did what I could."
"I had a lot of good luck."
"I'm surprised you're pleased."
"It could have gone better."
"It was a close call."
"Really? I didn't think things went all that well."

Learn to Apologize

Most mistakes are not catastrophic and beyond fixing, but the feelings they create—in you or in your boss—can be far more difficult to repair. When you make a mistake, therefore, it is crucial that you communicate right away.

1. Acknowledge the error.

2. Accept responsibility.

3. Apologize—briefly.

4. Offer suggestions for remedying the situation.

5. If you cannot offer solutions right away, promise to find them.

Time is of the essence. Report the error or snafu promptly. Avoid conveying a panicked frenzy, but do understand that it is far better that the news of *your* error come from you than from someone else or—even worse—as a result of your boss discovering it for himself. Nevertheless, be sure to take sufficient time to assess the full nature and degree of the error and to formulate solutions.

When you report the error, be sure that you:

- Deliver the facts. Endeavor to remain objective.

- Take responsibility. Don't point fingers.

- Don't beat yourself up—even as you accept responsibility.

- Provide solutions and fix-it procedures. These are what your boss wants to hear right now. He's not interested in watching you wallow in self-bestowed guilt.

Real World

Having reviewed the theory of communicating with your boss, put it to work. What follows are two scenarios that take place all the time between employees and their bosses, but that are especially important in challenging times.

"Routine" Salary Review

Yes, the quotation marks above are intended to be ironic. First, although a salary review may be *routinely* scheduled—perhaps at each anniversary of your employment—the event is never "routine" for you. You always need more money, right? Well, this is your chance to get it. Second, it is a mistake to regard any interchange with your boss as routine, and it is a very big mistake to regard *this* meeting that way. Third, when times are tough, the "routine" salary review can be a prelude to a salary *cut* or even a layoff. All you know for sure is that your raise is on the line. But you may have reason—good reason—to suspect another thing: *Your job is on the line.*

Don't give your boss an excuse to defer your raise, to cut your pay, or to lay you off. Go into the review with the goal of obtaining a raise. You may or may not get it. But you are not obliged to surrender, regardless of the outcome.

Understand that you are expected to make a case for getting a raise. You know why you need more money. Everything is expensive, and you want more of everything. This, however, is not the argument to make to your boss. In salary negotiation, never bring your needs into the discussion. Instead, make the negotiation about what you can deliver to satisfy your boss's needs.

Do your homework. You should walk into the review armed with two sets of data:

1. The highlights of your accomplishments over the preceding year. Emphasize numbers, dollars earned for the company, dollars saved for the company.

2. A review of what others, in similar positions, get paid—assuming that it is more than your present salary. This information is generally published by trade organizations in your field.

As always when you meet with the boss, you should approach this event not as an occasion to ask for something, but as a negotiation of value for value. Do enough research to form a firm idea of how much more money you can reasonably expect, but do not begin the discussion by stating a dollar amount. Skilled negotiators do not lay their cards faceup on the table. The number *you* start with automatically caps your salary for that year. Let your boss be the first to mention a number.

Work with the offer. Even if it is truly satisfactory, resist the temptation to accept it. It makes more sense to ask for more. Now is the time to make a counteroffer: "I appreciate the offer, but I believe the value I've delivered this past year—especially with regard to X, Y, and Z—merits more. This is the figure I was thinking of." Making a counteroffer will create a stronger bond between you and your boss than simply accepting the offer. It will present your picture of your own self-value.

Especially in troubled times, your boss may respond that she cannot give you any raise "at this time." Assuming you want to keep your job, respond by making the best of it for *now* while securing another salary review sooner rather than later: "I know times are tough, and, for the good of the company, I'm willing to continue at my present salary for now. When can we schedule another salary review?"

If your boss uses the occasion of a "routine" review to "offer" you a salary cut, you need to decide what is best for you. Remember, it is infinitely easier to go job hunting while you are employed than it is after you've been laid off. It is almost certainly in your best interest, therefore, to respond as positively as possible: "I know times are tough, and, for the good of the company, I'm willing to take the cut, but when can we schedule another salary review?" Do not express dismay. Do not threaten to look for another job. (You don't have to. Your boss probably assumes as much.) Make it clear that you will continue to work at a high level because you want to help put the company back into a position from which you can be compensated at a level you deserve.

Stepping Up

As with negotiating a raise, your objective in talking to your boss about a promotion is to demonstrate your value, not to demand something while offering nothing in return. If you think that the only time to bring up the subject is when business is going great, think again. It is true that, when business is low, getting either a raise or a promotion can be difficult—perhaps even impossible. But you may find that it is actually easier, in such times, to negotiate for a promotion than for a raise. Whereas a raise is a reward for value delivered, a promotion is not only a reward for *past* performance, but represents your proposal and promise to deliver even greater value in the future.

Avoid presenting the bid for promotion as a reward for your performance. Instead, frame it as a set of additional responsibilities you are willing to take on: more work, a bigger job, greater value, which you are prepared to deliver to the enterprise. Present the idea of a promotion as a proposal to deliver greater value for greater value received. Present it as a deal.

As when you negotiate for a raise, enter the discussion armed with a menu of your accomplishments expressed (to the degree possible) in money made and money saved for the firm. Use your performance in your present position as the basis from which to predict your even greater performance in the higher position.

Failure *Is* an Option

There is never any guarantee that you will get what you want from your boss, whether business is booming or not. So go ahead. Think of failure as an option—a perfectly viable option. Even if you fail to get the raise or promotion you want, the fact that you endeavored to negotiate for a raise or promotion is your vote of confidence in the future of the firm and an expression of your commitment to the company through thick and thin. It *will* satisfy your customer.

CHAPTER 9

HARD HEADS, HARD HEARTS, AND HARD ASSES

Earn a reputation for resolving conflict or, better yet, converting conflict into opportunity, and you are well on your way to making yourself an indispensable brand. The secret, as we've seen, is to focus on fixing problems instead of trying to fix people. The trouble is that workplace conflict is not always about problem issues. It's often created by problem people—folks who are just what the title of this chapter calls them. The good news is that they can be dealt with and dealt with so productively that you can advance your career while you do it.

Categorically Speaking

People can find many ways to make themselves difficult, but, in the workplace, most difficult people fall into one or more of five broad types, each of which calls for a different response from you. Knowing what to expect will help you to create satisfaction in even the most difficult people. Do this consistently and you'll not only dodge some potentially career-killing bullets, but earn a coveted place as the in-house snake charmer. Your goal is not to change the other person, but to create the conditions that will allow you to work productively with him.

1. The Bully

Bullies are not confined to the schoolyard, but are also commonly found in the workplace. The range of bullying behavior is broad. Hard cases bluster, bellow, and berate, whereas some bullies operate at a much lower pitch and subtler volume. Instead of using openly abrasive and abusive language, they find other ways of intimidating their colleagues. In all cases, however, the bully's objective is to make you feel inadequate and even downright inferior.

The abrasive and abusive bullies are easy to recognize. The subtler examples of the species require closer attention. They typically behave something like this: You champion a project and present it to your work group. Your expectation is that it will be discussed and debated on its merits. Instead, first to chime in is the bully: "Are you *serious* about this?" she says. "This is a joke, right?"

Two things are happening here:

- First, the bully is attempting to preempt any actual discussion of your proposal by doing what rhetoricians call "poisoning the well." That is, her mock questions make it difficult for anyone to support your project because, if they do, they're falling for a joke and thereby revealing themselves as foolish and probably incompetent. The bully is trying to render your proposal toxic before anyone actually evaluates it.

- Second, the bully is attempting to intimidate you into withdrawing your project. The verbal assault is aimed at demoralizing you, prompting you to emulate a turtle by pulling in your head, arms, and legs.

Presenting a project on its merits is demanding. You may be challenged and called on to defend it in detail. Hard as this may be, it's all fair, and you should accept it as part of your job. But enduring a verbal assault on you, an attack that bypasses the issue (the proposed project), is not part of your job, and you should not let it stand unchallenged.

Naturally, it can be hard to remain confident under an attack like this. That's the point of the tactic. The bully is playing a head game, seeking to psyche you out, demoralize you, and shut you up. Just keep in mind that the bully is armed with nothing but empty words and is up against the facts with which you are armed. Keep your cool, deploy your facts, and you should be able to pop the bully's verbal bubble.

By attacking you instead of the merits of your idea, proposal, or project, the bully is trying to move the battle to a field convenient to him. Don't move along with him. Don't respond to the bully's attack.

"Are you *serious* about this?" *seems* to demand an answer, but it's an illegitimate question. Therefore, ignore it. Blow right past it with the facts:

Bully: Are you *serious* about this?
You: The approach I'm proposing will save us XX percent in overhead costs.

Provided your facts are persuasive, they will make the bully's personal remarks appear to be exactly what they are. Not right, not wrong, just irrelevant.

If a bully had real substance to back himself up, he wouldn't resort to being a bully. Without substance, however, all he can do is play a role, and the role of bully, by its very nature, can never be a solo act. A bully cannot be a bully without a victim. Refuse to play *that* role, decline to be the victim, and the bully ends up as nothing more than someone making an unpleasant noise.

The following tactics should help you avoid, or stop playing victim to, the bully:

1. As much as possible, avoid dealing with or even talking to the bully. There is no rule that says you have to confront her on every conceivable occasion. Cut her out of your professional life as much as you can. Minimize all business with her.

2. See as little of the bully as you can manage. Use email instead of the phone or face-to-face contact.

3. When the curtain goes up on the bully's show, let the show go on while you step aside silently. Maintain eye contact and don't interrupt. When he gives you an opening, intrude with the facts and ignore the tirade. Don't ask him to "calm down," and don't admonish him: "There's no need for that kind of language." Instead, ignore the emotion and reiterate the facts: "As I was saying, two issues remain to be resolved . . ."

4. Don't argue. Don't shout. Don't threaten. But don't back down:

You: Ted, I need your sales report this afternoon.
Bully: Listen, I don't have time for that paperwork right now. I mean, how can you expect me to drop everything for busywork?
You: I understand, but I still need that report this afternoon.

Don't argue. Just assert—and reassert.

5. Whatever you feel, show no fear. In fact, show as little emotion as possible. Come across as bland, dead calm.

6. If the bully vents, let her. Then repeat the facts as necessary.

The bully wants a quick but decisive emotional skirmish. Deliver instead a slow war of attrition. Attacked with an outburst, respond with the facts. If you fail to stoke the emotional furnace, the fire is sure to die.

2. The Passive Aggressor

Passive-aggressive behavior is characterized by passively obstructionist resistance in the workplace. Passive-aggressive people typically procrastinate, sulk, and claim helplessness. They may come across as easygoing, perhaps even shy or meek, but they are keen saboteurs. If there is a single word to describe the passive-aggressive person in the workplace, it is *unreliable.* In fact, you can rely on the passive aggressor's unreliability. Require some important task to be performed, secure the passive aggressor's promise that he will complete it, walk away, return at the deadline, and the task, you will find, remains undone. On that you can rely. This is a problem whether you are in the position of supervising such a person or having to work with her on a task assigned by someone else.

When you confront the passive-aggressive subordinate or colleague about her failure to complete the assignment, she will reply, "Don't worry. I'm on it."

It still won't get done. Rely on it.

If you are in a supervisory position, avoid calling on the passive aggressor to perform mission-critical tasks. If possible, avoid teaming up with him. If you have no choice, however, resign yourself to monitoring and micromanaging the passive aggressor, riding him until he gets the work done. Run through this checklist:

- If you are assigning a task to a passive aggressor, draw up a timetable for every stage of the task and specify all requirements, with emphasis on outcome criteria.

- If you are teamed up with him, take charge early in the process. Put everything in writing, including the division of tasks and the timetable for completion.

- Keep tabs. Monitor progress. Obtain facts and figures, not assurances and reassurances.

- Send tickler emails that remind her of all deadlines and other requirements.

- Repeat instructions, objectives, and goals as often as necessary. If you are exasperated—and you will be—suck it up. Express no frustration.

Whether you are supervising or collaborating, address tangible behavior and the outcomes of that behavior. Control and modify these by using schedules, monitoring and evaluating progress on an ongoing basis, and repeating everything, including instructions, objectives, and goals.

3. The Chronic Complainer

There are productive complainers, and then there are complainers who channel all their productive energies into nonproductive whining. The first may get on your nerves, but if they also get the job done, count yourself lucky and let them whine on. The second, however, make your work harder and can even put your job in jeopardy to the extent that *your* job depends on *their* performance.

The usual MO of chronic complainers of the second kind is to use whining as a way to dodge work, including the assignments you give or on which the performance of you and your team relies. Most complaints boil down to one or both of the following:

1. "I can't do such-and-such because it (a) won't work or (b) it can't be done."

2. "I don't have the (a) time, (b) equipment, (c) personnel, or (d) training to do such-and such."

Take a deep, cleansing breath and proceed stepwise:

STEP 1: Determine if the complaint is based on reality. You may have a gut feeling that you're dealing with a work-dodging whiner, but you cannot proceed on that assumption before first evaluating the merit of the complaint. Maybe the assignment really is impossible. Maybe your department really does lack the tools or the personnel to do it. Determine this before proceeding.

STEP 2: As soon as you determine that you are dealing with an evasive complainer, cease all discussion of the merits of the complaint.

STEP 3: Express no sympathy for the complainer or her complaints.

STEP 4: Explain and emphasize the importance of doing the assignment or solving the problem.

STEP 5: Say that it is *necessary* to do or solve it.

STEP 6: Repeat Step 5.

STEP 7: This one is hard. Whether you are supervising the complainer or just trying to work with him, give him permission to fail. Tell him to tackle the assignment while also assuring him that you will evaluate the results and offer help if necessary. Explain that you understand the outcome may not be perfect, but you will work with him to make it come out right. Yes, this means that you are agreeing to take on extra work, but it may be your only hope of getting any usable work out of him.

4. The Schemer

Gossip can damage a career, but, usually, it's nothing more or less than a waste of what should be productive time. That's bad enough, but some people do use gossip and rumor with genuinely malicious intent, in an effort to damage you and thereby advance themselves. Some of these backstabbers are sufficiently skilled to attack with total stealth. Even the indispensable are not immune, but as with most ills in life, the proverbial ounce of prevention is worth more than a few pounds of cure. Ward off would-be schemers by:

- Cultivating good corporate karma, as discussed in Chapter 5. The Italian political philosopher Niccolò Machiavelli wrote that it was better to be feared than loved. In the modern workplace, however, *best* of all is to be *liked*—by everyone. Make that your mission. Practice empathy.

- Engage those you work with on a fully human level. They're people, not cogs. Talk to them about their lives, ambitions, interests, and dreams. Talk—but spend more time listening.

- Assemble a coterie of allies. Network internally (see Chapter 7) as well as externally. The time to do this is *all* of the time. Don't wait until you are under attack.

- As you would not want to be the subject of malicious gossip, do not engage in malicious gossip about anyone else.

- Keep your chin up and your nose down. Stay busy and look busy. Perform with excellence and create satisfaction. Make yourself unmistakably valuable through what you produce.

If, despite your vigilance, you find a shiv in your back, you'd better pull it out fast. No law says you have to confront the schemer. Instead, focus on damage control and repair. For instance, if you discover false rumors about you, respond with the truth. As with most potentially career-damaging conflicts, facts, issues, and outcomes speak louder than secondhand "information" and opinion.

Damage control and repair are not always sufficient to stop the mischief of a schemer, especially a persistent one. The first judgment call you'll have to make is whether or not to get your boss involved. The decision depends in part on your relationship with her. If you can approach her as one team member to another and present the situation as a problem that hurts the team, seeking intervention in this way will probably prove helpful. The downside of going to your boss, however, is real—and potentially damaging to your job. Even if she intervenes against your antagonist, you may end up looking incapable of handling the situation yourself. Your boss and others may recognize that the "other guy started it," but, fair or not, you'll be tagged as part of a problem. Even in the best of times, but especially during hard times, you want to be identified solely, solidly, and exclusively as part of the solution.

If at all feasible, then, deal with the schemer directly.

1. Ask him for a meeting. Somewhere outside of the office is best. Invite him out for coffee or lunch. The only venue to avoid is an impromptu hallway confrontation. Make it a "relaxed" but planned business meeting.

2. Broach the issues—or the purported issues—instead of challenging the person: "I've been hearing a buzz to the effect that you have identified some problems with the XYZ project I'm working on. I'm at a loss as to what these could be. Can you share your insight? Help me out?"

3. Leave the "gotcha!" attitude in your desk drawer. Just let the schemer struggle with the issues.

4. If, in response to your request for factual clarification, the schemer folds—"I don't know what you've heard, but I haven't told anybody about any problems"—ask for his cooperation in stopping the loose talk: "I'm sure glad to hear that. Do you have any idea who's spreading these rumors? I'd like to put a stop to them. I hope you'll help."

5. If the schemer has any issues to discuss, do discuss them. Don't respond with anger. Listen. Maybe there is even something of value in what she has to say.

6. After you have talked, act to reshape the schemer's future behavior: "Thanks for talking to me, Marilyn. In the future, I hope you'll feel that you can come straight to me if you have a suggestion or a problem with something I've done." Leave the discussion here, looking toward the future. Do *not* tell the schemer that her rumor-mongering has made you feel bad. To do so would be to hand her a victory.

5. The Poacher

No scheme is more common in the workplace than credit grabbing and idea stealing. Typically, the poacher listens to your casual discussion of an idea—he may even pick your brain in a seemingly collegial manner—then, next thing you know, he presents it or a close cousin to it as his own work.

Teamwork and collaboration are the hallmarks of most modern businesses. You have to share your ideas. Intellectual ownership and intellectual sharing are two sides of the same coin—the coin that buys your way into job security and career advancement. Go ahead and share, but protect yourself against poachers by taking the following steps:

- Commit your idea to writing *before* you discuss it with anyone. Date the writing. Store one original draft on a hard drive and on whatever backup you have available, including (if your company's security policies permit) a portable drive or thumb drive that you control completely.

- Distribute the idea, dated, with a note that it is a draft to which you are seeking input. Specify a deadline for all comments. Specify a date by which you plan to issue a final draft.

- Devote careful thought to your choice of collaborative partners. Don't broadcast your draft to all and sundry. Everyone who receives the draft should know the names of the other recipients. Caution all recipients not to share the draft with others.

If, despite your precautions, you suddenly hear your idea spoken in the voice of another, take action. Often, the poacher boldly presents *your* idea in a group meeting, in your very presence. He is betting that you will say nothing. See to it that he loses the bet: "Ben, isn't this the concept I presented to you on Monday? I sent it to George at that time, too." You may get some excuse or an outright denial. If you do, persist politely: "It *isn't* my concept? But how is what you're presenting different from what we discussed on Monday?"

Nail him.

And if you happen to be the "George" in this exchange, it is in your best interest to ensure that credit is given where credit is due. "Ben, that sounds like the idea you, Sarah, and I talked about last week. It's Sarah's idea, isn't it?"

It's Just Business

We all know what Ben Franklin said about certainty. It consisted exclusively of death and taxes. Had he given the matter a bit more thought, he would surely have added "and hard heads, hard hearts, and hard asses."

Difficult people are a fact of life, especially business life, where livelihoods are at stake, resources are inherently limited, and competitive passions can run high. Accept difficult people as you accept any other feature of your profession. Be as positive as possible. Formulate a strategy, and decide what results you want to achieve instead of just grimly anticipating an onslaught of bad feelings. *Feelings* will come and go. *Results* are what everybody in the organization is looking for. Do what you must to give them the results that demonstrate your value to the enterprise.

PART THREE

Holding On and Breaking Through

Rising in your career begins with just holding on, especially when times are tough. So Part Three opens with "A Handbook of Hazards." Let's call them career kryptonite—the workplace pitfalls that can hold you back, get you canned right now, and even cripple your future. The truths presented in Chapter 10 may be ugly, but the advice on handling them is no-nonsense. You'll learn to cope with the worst of the bad stuff and, better still, avoid it in the first place. Chapter 11 takes you to the place where "just holding on" becomes "climbing to the top." It introduces you to everything you need to know about networking. Here is a toolbox to help you build, maintain, and expand your career network both online and in real life. The final chapter in Part Three and in this book takes you out and up. After all, the goal of making yourself indispensable in the workplace is not just to stay put. Even in the hardest of times, making a living should be about more than just survival. The attitudes, skills, and perceptions you develop about and around yourself belong to *you*. Fully portable, they are yours to take with you to a new position, a new employer, a better job, a bigger career.

CHAPTER 10

A HANDBOOK OF HAZARDS

Faster than a speeding bullet, more powerful than a locomotive, able to leap tall buildings at a single bound, and destined to become the most popular and enduring of American superheroes, Superman debuted in *Action Comics* #1 in June of 1938. That the Man of Steel's emergence coincided with the still-lingering Great Depression, the rise of the "great dictators" in Europe and Japan, and the international anxiety of gathering war clouds was no coincidence. Frightened people were hungry for a role model possessed of super strength, super ability, and superpowers. To the citizens of crime-plagued Metropolis, Superman quickly made himself indispensable. And just as no Hitler or Mussolini could hurt him, so no boss could fire him. If he was fearless, he had good reason to be. He was invulnerable.

Well, not really.

At least since the days of Achilles, weavers of myth have understood that invulnerability makes for dull stories. So Achilles had a bum heel, and Superman has his kryptonite. Chemically speaking, kryptonite is what happened when Superman's home planet exploded. All of the atomic elements of Krypton—that was the name of the planet—fused into kryptonite, chunks of which were scattered throughout the universe, some even falling to Earth as meteorites. The substance comes in five varieties—red, gold, blue, white, and green—of which green kryptonite is fatal to Superman.

What does this comic book stuff have to do with you? Read on.

The Moral of Kryptonite

Kryptonite made the Superman story a lot more interesting and durable, while loading it with a moral as old as the tale of Achilles and myriad other mythic heroes: You may be very hard to kill, but you are not unkillable.

Born on Krypton, a planet with a red sun, the infant Superman was rocketed to Earth by his parents in an effort to save him as his birth planet writhed in its geological death throes. He thus grew into young manhood under the Earth's yellow sun, which conferred on him his extraordinary powers, including invulnerability to everything except the radiation of kryptonite. Harmless under Krypton's red sun and harmless to earthlings, the stuff is lethal to any Kryptonian dwelling under the yellow sun of Earth.

The moral of kryptonite? The very assets that make you an exceptional achiever, all those high-ticket "transferable skills" we talked about in Part One, can also be the liabilities that bring you down.

Consider: The plodding, clock-punching conformist may be doomed to a lackluster career and, insofar as he is perceived as an employment commodity, a generic plug to fit a generic socket, he's liable to be among the first to be "let go" in a recession, business downturn, downsizing, or general belt tightening. Even in boom times, his prospects for advancement are limited. You don't want to be this guy.

But also consider: The boldly ambitious striver who lifts her head high above the crowd runs the risk of getting it lopped off—in good times or bad.

There is a fine line separating attractive self-confidence from obnoxious arrogance. Narrow, too, is the border between a productively decisive approach to business and impulsive recklessness. What raises you above the level of an expendable, interchangeable commodity also renders you potentially vulnerable to the effects of the envy and insecurity of others. The most elementary of business principles tells us that there is no reward without risk. Successful people possess a willingness to take risks. Yet it is not always easy to see the difference between a calculated risk and a foolish gamble.

Superman cannot fight kryptonite and he cannot always avoid it. All he can do is stay aware and wary of its existence. Through self-awareness and strategic vigilance, he cannot eliminate the hazard, but he can manage it.

In hard, scary times, we are all tempted to keep our heads down, to blend in, to do anything but stick our necks out. World War II's legendary General George Patton saw this phenomenon in combat. Under heavy fire, soldiers were taught to stop advancing and dig in, hunkering down in foxholes. Patton argued that this did nothing more than create the illusion of safety. In fact, he believed, that the "safety" of the foxhole transformed men in motion, an army advancing against the enemy, into sitting ducks. You don't have to be a combat veteran to know that a stationary target is a lot easier to hit than a moving one.

Although it feels safer, sitting in a foxhole is more dangerous than advancing against the enemy. If your object is to emulate a superhero, to become indispensable in the workplace, you cannot avoid risk by cowering in the foxhole of mediocre conformity. But neither can you willfully ignore the hazards of standing out. You need to understand the dangers of allowing self-confidence to become blind arrogance, of allowing drive and decisiveness to become reckless action on impulse, and of allowing risk taking to become nothing more than a go-for-broke crap shoot. Like Superman's kryptonite, the hazards are always there. You cannot eliminate them. But you can manage the risks by preparing carefully before acting, by being mindful of the feelings and needs of others, and by always assessing with realistic objectivity the proportion of risk to reward before making any decision.

Danger Signs

Has any of this ever happened to you?

- You expected and you believe that you deserved a promotion, but it was given to a coworker who, in your objective judgment, was significantly less qualified than you.

- People who used to ask your advice no longer do.

- In a meeting, you find yourself under a barrage of unwarranted criticism.

- You aren't invited to the boss's pool party. (She says it was an "oversight" and apologizes—more or less.)

- You've become the subject of office gossip.

- People randomly ask you, "Is there anything wrong?"

- You are being scapegoated, blamed for snafus that could not possibly have been your fault.

- "Friends" are no longer very friendly.

- Your ability to put together ad hoc work groups and project teams has diminished or evaporated entirely. You discover that you can no longer rely on the cooperation and goodwill of your colleagues.

- Email queries and requests go unanswered. You have to nudge and nag.

Climb Out of the Foxhole

If any of these signs seem chillingly familiar to you, fight your impulse to press yourself deeper into your foxhole. It's time to stand up and move forward; make yourself harder to hit.

Review Chapter 6 and get yourself into shape as a fully qualified office diplomat. Isolation is not just the enemy of advancement, it's the first step out the door. The time for greater engagement in the politics of the office is precisely when you feel yourself coming under assault.

When you feel yourself being yanked out of the loop, get yourself back in by making yourself more influential. The more influential you can make yourself, the more powerful you will be perceived to be and, as a result, the more powerful you will actually become. You're not just saving yourself, you're advancing yourself.

Sell Your Influence

Start by selling your influence to others. The more ideas and initiatives you sell to others, especially to bosses, the more influential you will become. The most influential people are those most thoroughly woven into the workplace fabric.

- **Begin with one idea or proposal.** First identify someone in your office who has the power to help you. Use this person as a lever on which you can lift your proposal. Sell it to him, and he will sell it to others. Promoting an idea to an influential person multiplies your influence, just as a lever multiplies the effect of your arm muscle, even if you're far from possessing superhuman strength.

- **Sell your idea by selling its benefits.** Show how the idea directly benefits the person you are trying to influence. Let's say you have an idea for starting a special customer support group. You identify Claire, your immediate supervisor, as the person who wields the necessary clout to get your proposal a hearing with the people who have the power to make the project happen. You sell her on the benefits: "Claire, this customer support group will certainly gain *you* a stronger voice with upper management."

- **Create a deed by means of pronoun.** No idea sells easier than one the other guy thinks he already owns. As you begin to get buy-in from the person whose support you seek, start referring to the proposal as "our" concept rather than "my" concept.

- **Recruit your critics.** Instead of deflecting, turning away from, or becoming discouraged by whatever resistance you meet, recruit your critics to your cause. "Claire, your criticism has given me food for thought. I need your input to develop the support group further so that we can make it work." If you can't beat 'em, make 'em join you.

Make—or Remake—Friends

Cultivate warm personal relationships with the people who hold the major power and influence in your office. If you are finding that people seem to be drifting away from you, work at strengthening, even rebuilding relations.

- Keep your efforts positive. Do not ask if anything is wrong. Do not imply that you think something may be wrong.

- Try an invitation to lunch: "Fred, how about lunch? It's been awhile."

- If lunch feels to you like too big a step, make a more casual offer: "Fred, I'm on the way to the break room. Can I bring you back a cup of coffee?"

- Whether at lunch, over coffee, or during some other spontaneous moment you make happen, ask a question about something of interest to the other person: "Is your son still into soccer big-time?" "How's that 1967 'project Pontiac' coming along?" "Have you talked to Bonnie [a mutual friend] lately?" Keep the focus off yourself and on the other person.

- Cultivate, don't plow. No need to push or advance an agenda. You are creating—or restoring—a friendly, collegial climate in which others see you as something more than the occupant of a cubicle.

Wake Up to Ethics

The opening decade of the twenty-first century is littered with the wreckage of ethical failure in business. Adelphia, Tyco, WorldCom, and Enron are the top-of-mind examples of ethical implosion, and the scandals associated with them were so big that, at long last, managers at every level have embraced "business ethics" not just as something nice to have once you've hit your bottom-line numbers, but as an absolutely essential element in commerce. Ethics is not just for Boy Scouts and Girl Scouts anymore. These days, not only is a reputation for unimpeachable ethical conduct a real employment positive, any whiff of unethical action shoots a bright green kryptonite ray right between the alleged perpetrator's eyes.

Unethical action: We're not talking about Bernie Madoff criminality. You feel overworked and underpaid, right? So, on occasion, you order office supplies on the company's dime and use them at home. Everyone does it, don't they?

That's not the question to ask. The question is *Are you a thief?* And the answer is *In this case, yes, you are a thief.*

While it's not likely that your boss will call 911 if she discovers what you've done, there is a very real chance that she could fire you, especially if, in hard times, she's looking for an excuse to fire people. At the very least, she'll remember you, come salary review time, not as the sales rep who consistently hits her numbers, but as the young woman who stole a stapler and three reams of 24-pound bright-white paper.

Want more?

- Back from a business trip, you sit down to make out your expense report. Earlier, the talk at lunch was about how *absolutely everybody* in the company pads expense reports. "It's S.O.P. It's expected. Practically mandatory!" So you follow the crowd, adding a few dollars in the tips and miscellaneous categories. Thief.

- It takes you four uninterrupted, hard-driving, top-quality hours to finish a client's job. You had estimated six. But you're good at what you do—and fast. The client approved the estimate, so you bill him for the six hours he was expecting. Thief.

Unethical conduct is unethical, regardless of how you try to justify it, regardless of how many others engage in it, and even if you're absolutely convinced you can get away with it. The job-killing, maybe even career-killing hazards of unethical conduct include:

- The possibility of getting caught and the consequences thereof.

- Contributing to the creation of an unethical environment. This pollution tends to spread throughout the organization, then into the business community, and out to the community generally. You may not get singled out, but, sooner or later, the reputation of your firm will begin to suffer and, with it, yours.

Make it your business to know, understand, and abide by your company's ethical policies. Then step beyond mere compliance. Make your ethical conduct a positive, value-added benefit you offer to your customers, both internal (colleagues, subordinates, and bosses) and external. Sell ethics. Brand yourself as ethical. There is security and value in the proposition.

How to Stop Making Yourself Dispensable

There are many ways to build a career and, unfortunately, more than a few ways to kill one. You've been reading a lot about making yourself indispensable. Now let's look at the flip side. If you recognize yourself in any of what follows, make the necessary course corrections.

"I'm Not Interested in Being a 'Team Player'"

President George W. Bush famously boasted "I don't do nuance." If you pride yourself on being an office maverick and therefore think that being a "team player" is the same as following the herd into the pen of conformity, you apparently don't "do nuance" either. The differences may not be glaringly obvious, but they are essential to survival as well as advancement.

The least vulnerable, most indispensable employees are those who fit in while standing out. This requires being a team player without surrendering your individual voice, creativity, and judgment. Keep these, but always exercise them for the benefit of the team. Since you're part of the team, maybe even leading the team, the benefits will be yours as much as anyone else's.

Getting yourself branded as *not a team player* is not the same as branding yourself an "out-of-the-box thinker," a "real original," or a "creative individual." Those things are positives. They're assets, whereas "not a team player" is a liability. Period. Get this label plastered across your forehead, and you become toxic.

Choosing between teamwork and individual achievement/individual recognition is a false choice. The *real* choice is deciding to work in a team context but to work so hard and so smart that your individual efforts are recognized and rewarded. The concept is hardly a new one. Just think of the stars on any baseball, football, basketball, or other sports team. Don't picture teamwork as a mass grave, but as a stage with more than one spotlight. Building, using, and exhibiting *your* transferable skills in a team setting means nothing more or less than ensuring that you never give the appearance that your only objective is looking out for yourself. Your value is *your* value, which is measured as your value to *others*. This is the essence of teamwork, and it will keep you employed while also propelling you upward.

"That's Not My Job"

It's fine and dandy to understand your job, including the duties outlined in the official job description. Just don't get too comfortable with what's written down. Whatever your set duties and responsibilities, always look beyond them for new opportunities and fresh ways to productively expand your position. Get above and beyond the entry-level minimums as soon as possible.

As you should not define yourself by your job description, don't let others define you this way either. Volunteer. Take on extra work in related areas. Demonstrate your fearless will to seize the initiative. Settle back into your job description as if it were a lounge chair, and you may find it very hard to get up—ever.

If you've come in at the entry level, do your job and express no discontent with the job. Never give the impression that you regard it as nothing more than a stepping-stone. (Bosses hate that.) Nevertheless, promote your-self. Make it clear that you are willing to pay your dues, but point out the untapped skills you have to offer. Present them to your boss as a value-added proposition: "I'd like to expand my responsibilities to include research. You know I have training in that area. Why not let me give you the benefit of it? I can guarantee that the fact-checking you hired me for will get done in full and on schedule, but I know you can use another set of brains on research. I'm willing to put in the extra time."

"There's No Hurry"

Procrastination is a common problem. It's also a common cause of unem-ployment and underemployment. Take deadlines seriously. Why do you think *dead* is part of the word?

Procrastinating not only risks late delivery, it also courts compromised quality. Rushed work usually looks rushed. Double-checking doesn't get done. Proofreading doesn't get done. Fact-checking doesn't get done. Ram-ifications don't get considered. Checklists go unchecked. The result may be on time—barely—but if you're out of breath and your work is sloppy, second-rate, or just plain bad, what's your message and what's the point?

"I'm Working till I Drop"

It is important to look busy, especially these days. But, in the end, it's a high-quality work product your employer wants and is willing to reward, not the humming and hopping appearance of production. A big part of maintaining this quality is avoiding the mental and physical exhaustion known as burn-out. You wouldn't purposely run a machine until it breaks down. Why risk doing the same with yourself?

Get to know yourself. There is a point at which every worker experiences diminishing returns. For example, work forty-hour weeks, and you might (in this economy) barely hang on to your job. Work sixty hours, and you may achieve a level of production that will make you too valuable to fire. Work seventy hours a week, and you may find your production diminishing, if not in quantity, then in quality. Maybe you'll look busier, and maybe your boss will praise your initiative, but when you start fumbling because you are too burned-out to remember your own name, you are not going to make the impression you want to make.

Take a breath.

Inventory your work and personal life. Slow down just to the point of optimum production. Maintain yourself at least as well as you would maintain a fine and expensive piece of machinery.

"I Know My Job"

Failing to keep your technical skills current is a job and career killer. At the very least, you need to stay on par with your colleagues as well as those coming up from the ranks or out of the schools. Preferably, you'll want to build on your platform of experience not just to keep up but to get and stay ahead of the others.

Whatever else you may have to offer, the faintest whiff of obsolescence will cause all around you to hold their noses. Stay up-to-date in technical skills, business skills, and whatever other skills your job and industry require. Look for ways to expand and advance your skill set. If you can be the one to introduce technical innovation to your shop, you will greatly increase your perceived and actual value to your current employer and others.

"I'm Efficient. What Else Do You Want from Me?"

It can be fatal to confuse efficiency with effectiveness. Communicating by email is efficient, but it is not always as effective as walking down the hall for a face-to-face with the head of production. The ease and, yes, the efficiency of digital communications make the effort and apparent inefficiency of face-to-face meetings more effective than ever. "Face time" has become a precious commodity in business.

Want to give more of yourself? Then give yourself IRL (in real life).

"I Did It, I Did It, I Did It"

One instance of a failure to share credit for collaborative or team achievements can tear down months or years of goodwill and corporate karma.

Sharing credit where credit is due makes you a great guy in the eyes of bosses and in the hearts of those with whom you work and on whom your further success depends. Grabbing all the glory will leave you, in the end, empty-handed.

"Modesty Forbids Me"

The only blunder more quickly fatal to a career than failing to give credit where credit is due is failing to give yourself credit when it is due to you. Self-promotion is the most important kind of promotion because no one knows the scope, depth, and benefit of your achievements better than you do. Write, collect, and share case studies, promotion bulletins, and similar documents to illustrate the magnitude of what you have achieved not just for yourself but for the benefit of the enterprise. Inform everyone you work with, including bosses, colleagues, subordinates, and clients. Heighten your visibility.

Self-promotion requires a record of genuine achievement. There is no substitute for actually creating measurable value for your employer. Want to keep your job? Want to advance in it? Stand on the platform of the value you produce and make yourself famous.

"Networking Is Just a Lot of Busywork"

Until you actually start getting clients, promotions, and jobs through networking, you may find it hard to believe that networking will get you anywhere. You've got too much on your plate to add a heaping helping of networking just now, right?

Everyone knows that networking can be an aid to finding a job, but too many of us shut down our job-hunting networks once we've found employment. Like failing to practice self-promotion, failing to maintain and grow a network is a career-stunting mistake. The next chapter will help you get plugged in—and stay connected.

CHAPTER 11

THE INDISPENSABLE NETWORK

Maybe you were recruited for your job. Maybe you found it through an ad online or in a professional journal. Maybe. But, more likely, you landed it through networking. You might not have called the process by that name. You just "asked around." You "contacted your friends." You "talked to people in the business." Well, guess what? *That's* networking.

Networking works. If you're sure you didn't get your job by networking, ask half a dozen of your coworkers how they got theirs. I bet at least four will have a networking story to tell. But ask them if they are still active networkers, and you're likely to get a yes from no more than two.

When something is proven to work, it's plain common sense to continue doing it. Yet most people, once they get a job, slack off on maintaining their network, let alone devoting real effort to expanding it. The truth is that maintaining and adding to your contacts *after* you are hired is critical to the continuing success of your career. Not only does networking help keep you current on the buzz in your field, it gives you people to call when you need advice, it sets you up as a source of authoritative information and counsel, and, while making you known beyond your own department or company, it promotes your company to others. Carry the corporate banner higher and farther than anybody else, and you are bound to start looking indispensable.

Where to Start

How do you start a network?

Begin by opening up to the people around you. Get to know your colleagues and coworkers as people, not just as holders of a job title. Let them get to know you the same way. Ask for information and help when you need it. Give information and help when you're asked. When you're invited to lunch, to an office event, to a party, accept—every single time, if you can. Expand your circle of contacts in any way that comes naturally to you.

These days, you don't have to be at work or even out and about to start building a network.

- Get familiar with the many social and professional websites— Facebook, LinkedIn, and the rest—that are freely available (we'll talk about them more shortly).

- Identify and explore blogs and websites directly related to your industry.

- Set up your own page on Facebook, LinkedIn, and other sites. Consider blogging.

- Check out the resources offered by your college alumni association, join professional organizations, and attend professional conferences and conventions.

- At office and industry or professional gatherings, don't be a spectator. Talk to people. Arm yourself with business cards and pass them out—generously.

- Make contacts everywhere you go.

Be a Friend

Making contacts wherever you go does not require sleazy, shallow self-promotion. Networking doesn't have to be a robotic ritual limited to exchanging business cards (but *do* exchange them). Effective networking can begin with nothing more or less than behaving like a friend:

- Whenever you communicate with a business contact—client, colleague, vendor, whoever—ask how that person is doing. Demonstrate a genuine interest in the person's life and concerns. At first, you may feel a little awkward doing this. You may even feel that you are faking it. But get accustomed to asking after the welfare of others, and not only will you soon find it coming naturally, you'll be surprised at just how interested you really are in the lives of those with whom you do business.

- Stay in touch. A big part of networking is doing nothing more than letting people know what you're up to. Consider circulating an occasional personal "newsletter" to your circle of contacts. Let people know what you're doing. Let them know what you have to offer *them.*

- Build a database of important days. Record your key contacts' birthdays and anniversaries. Send cards or celebratory emails or make a friendly call on that important day. Season's greetings are also always welcome.

- Don't let growing your network cause you to neglect those who are already in it. Maintain as well as expand.

Invest time and interest in people, and they will very likely return the investment—with interest. That is the payoff of networking.

Get Out There

Accept every work-related invitation you possibly can. Attend every convention or professional get-together that is open to you. If you're lucky, your company will pay your way to conventions, conferences, and the like, but you should also consider attending some on your own dime. Introduce yourself. Talk and, just as important, listen. Take names. Collect business cards.

Don't limit yourself to attending established events. Consider getting together with colleagues in your office and your industry on a regular but informal basis—perhaps a monthly gathering at a favorite after-work watering hole.

Take a Social Inventory

Even if you don't consider yourself a "joiner," you are probably active in a number of social organizations—perhaps your church, synagogue, or mosque; the local PTA or PTO; a service organization, or a sports club. Use such venues to communicate to others your passion for what you do for a living. You never know what connections you may make.

Work the Room

When you are at a social or professional event, make the very most of it. If you don't consider yourself a natural-born mingler, you're hardly alone. Most people feel awkward and uncomfortable in a room full of strangers. You *can* learn to convert those strangers into potentially productive professional contacts, and with practice the process becomes easier.

Get Yourself into the Zone

Mingling productively requires energy. The first step is to jettison all thoughts and attitudes that sap energy and thus drive you back into your shell. You may be afraid that you don't know enough to engage in an intelligent professional conversation with higher-ups. You may feel that it is futile to try to impress a major industry figure at a convention because you're only one of hundreds trying to do the same. You may simply think that you're just not a "people person."

Go ahead, say these things to yourself. Then set them aside and forget them. They don't matter. Instead, latch onto the positives:

- Don't worry about talking about yourself. Get others to talk about *themselves*. It's what most people like to do anyway. Ask questions. Begin with the obvious: "What do you do at ABC Company?"

- Show interest in who a person is and what she does, and you will make her feel good. Such interest is flattering, and everyone relishes flattery. Make a person feel good, and he will reciprocate with sincere interest in you and what you have to say.

While you're at it, why not rethink the whole concept of "a roomful of strangers"? The chances are good that, in any industry or professional meeting, you will run into people you know, at least slightly—even if you've only seen them at the last meeting. Make even this slender relationship the basis of a good conversation: "Hi, I'm George Perkins from ABC Company. I've seen you at these meetings before, but I've never had a chance to introduce myself. Tell me, what do you do?"

Even if this is the very first time you have met the person to whom you are about to speak, he's still not a *total* stranger. Assuming you are in the same industry, you already have certain interests in common. Probably, you're both trying to get ahead in your careers. And at the very least, the two of you have one mission in common: You are both trying to get through an awkward meeting with a stranger!

Break the Ice

A conversation starts with someone. Might as well be you.

- **Take the initiative.** Approach others and introduce yourself. Share a piece of information aimed at revealing a common interest: "This is my first time at one of these meetings. Are you new, too?" If the answer is yes, you've got something in common. If the answer is no, you can ask for advice: "What presentations are usually the most useful?"

- **Devote most of the conversation to listening.** Pick up on the other person's interests and concerns. If you make these the subject of the conversation, you will be sure to develop and hold the other person's attention.

Be Prepared

Spontaneity is a generally overrated quality. If you worry about getting tongue-tied when you are expected to start a conversation with a stranger, come well prepared with a self-introduction that you have thoroughly rehearsed beforehand. What you say need occupy only ten seconds or so, and the first couple of those seconds are always taken up with giving your name. Say who you are, what you do, and ask a question: "Hi, I'm Rebecca Smith, sales rep with ABC Widgets. Who are you and what interests you today?"

Social Media

Not surprisingly, the Inter*net* has proven to be a natural medium for *net*working. In fact, these days, when the conversation turns to "networking," most people are likely to assume the subject is Facebook, LinkedIn, and the like.

Social media—websites designed to bring people together—can put your personal and professional network on steroids, at least in terms of amassing sheer head count. Take advantage of what the Internet offers, but don't make the mistake of assuming that digital networking is a substitute for networking face–to-face.

- Use social media to expand your network.

- Use social media to keep in touch with people you meet personally.

- Use social media to identify individuals you should try to meet face to face.

- But however much you use social media, keep making important contacts face to face.

Many industries and professions have spawned their own networking sites. Make it your business to get to know them and to use them. Let's survey here some of the most popular sites most commonly used in business networking.

MySpace

One of the early forces in social media, MySpace is now mostly a networking tool for younger people. If you are in a business that needs to reach a youthful target audience, MySpace is very much worth pursuing. If not, however, you probably won't find it a useful networking tool.

LinkedIn and Xing

LinkedIn has become the most commonly used business social media tool in the United States. As of summer 2010, there are some 60 million profiles on LinkedIn. The site is not only geographically American, it is culturally American, so if what you really need is a *global* networking presence, be sure to check out Xing as well. Created in Germany in 2003, Xing is almost certainly the largest international business social networking site, with more than eight million users as of 2010. Xing is available in 16 languages.

Many people who use LinkedIn have a thousand connections or more—a network with more than a thousand nodes. Does this mean they have personal relationships with more than a thousand people? Almost certainly not. Indeed, the American anthropologist Robin Dunbar theorized in the 1990s that the human brain is physically incapable of truly knowing more than about 150 people. But that doesn't mean that the 850 or so other connections many professionals have are meaningless. They are all potentially valuable in business, either directly or indirectly. When a professional contact asks you if you know anything about XYZ, you may not be able to answer yes, but, thanks to LinkedIn, you *may* be able to answer, "I know someone who does. Let me put you in touch with her."

You may feel the urge to expand your LinkedIn network by leaps and bounds; however, beware of growing any network indiscriminately. Do you really want random connections with hordes of people you've never even heard of? When you connect with someone on LinkedIn, that person will have access to your business relationships. Exercise common sense when you decide whether to accept or reject a request for a connection. If you don't know the person or someone connected to the person, or if the person is not with a company you are interested in, consider turning down the invitation to connect.

- Ask yourself why you should abandon in the social networking arena the kinds of criteria and standards you live by when you network face to face. In real life, you probably would not recommend someone to your valued contacts unless you knew the person in some significant way. Protect your reputation and your relationships in the digital realm as vigilantly as you do in real life.

As you become accustomed to LinkedIn, you will find yourself using it to obtain appointments and to locate potentially valuable business contacts just about anywhere. The site will give you a lot of information about people you want to get to know. It will enable you to find everyone in a given company who has a LinkedIn profile. You can even ask one of your personal connections to introduce you electronically to one of their connections.

Twitter

Twitter is a social networking site that allows users to broadcast brief chunks of information and publish them either to an RSS feed, email, or a number of other applications. The bottom line for Twitter is that it's fun, informal, and less intrusive than other forms of casual communication. Twitter is a nearly effortless platform for sharing information—though most users read rather than contribute Tweets.

As of summer 2010, it had about 105 million users, but adds thousands daily. Because users are limited to 140 characters per Tweet, the medium calls for brevity, which, under the best of circumstances, forces users to think before they Tweet.

The trick to using Twitter effectively as a networking tool is to avoid being boring:

- Make at least some of your conversations relevant to something other than yourself or your business. If you're connected to a large number of businesspeople, the content stream can start feeling generic as everyone writes about his or her job.

- Just because you can update every thought in your head and every move you make doesn't mean you necessarily should.

- Make your Tweets personal. Make them special. Talk about your family, your coworkers, your charitable work, and the not-for-profit organizations your company supports. Make your Tweets real, and you will create real relationships.

Although posts must be brief, Twitter enables you to find detailed information on a variety of subjects.

- The best Twitter posters include a URL to an interesting website or article. The 140-character Tweet allows you to know what the message is about and then gives you the option to take a deeper dive via the link.

- Learn how to use hash tags. Preceded by # (the "hash symbol"), a hash tag is usually a single word or two words joined together, representing a subject or an event. If you are attending an event that furnishes a hash tag, you can use the tag to mark your Tweets from the event, thereby providing your network with a way to get a glimpse of unfolding events. Provide members of your network with high-value information (that is, news they can use), and your value as an influential member of your business or professional community rises. This, in turn, puts you on your way to being indispensable.

- Tweet to be retweeted. Those who receive your Tweets can pass them along to a larger population. If you are providing useful and compelling information, people in your network will "retweet" your original posting. This is a great way to heighten your visibility throughout any business community.

On the Job

Don't confine your network to people outside of your current place of employment. Reach out as well to people in your company but outside of your department. And there's no rule against networking with the guy in the very next cubicle, either. The more you are connected to your industry, your company, and your department, the less isolated you are. Avoiding isolation is essential to both advancement and survival.

The Little-Known Art of Internal Networking

Mention *networking*, and most people think of attending various "events" or getting on a social media website. It is rare that businesspeople consider the power of internal networking, networking within the walls of their own offices.

Everyone in your organization represents a potential network of relationships. Get to know everyone, from the receptionist to the CEO. Each person is a nexus of relationships and potentially valuable connections. Here are some ideas for reaching out:

- Make it a habit to eat in the break room.

- Gather a group for lunch.

- Take a deep breath and ask your boss to lunch.

- Organize a company softball team—or other *fun* special interest group.

- Organize a company picnic.

The idea is to create opportunities to interact outside of the office. This will help you get to know, on a human level, those you work with, and it will help them to know you.

To Expand Your World, Shrink It

In big organizations, you may find it difficult to organize the kind of out-of-office experiences that provide the best networking opportunities. Try these tactics:

- Work with Human Resources to organize a company-wide outing.

- Propose creating a company directory with headshots and bios; this could be done on the company website at virtually no cost.

- Work with others to organize dedicated company-wide networking opportunities.

- Either create or contribute to an existing or departmental newsletter, online or in print, which regularly spotlights individual employees.

Take the lead in bringing your department or company together into a genuine community, and you will not only be networking with the people who call the shots in your organization, you will become the hub of the corporate wheel—an indispensable part of the enterprise.

CHAPTER 12

STEPPING OUT AND STEPPING UP

The goal of making yourself indispensable in the workplace is not just to stay put, but to move on and move up. Even in hard times, making a living should be about more than just survival. The attitudes, skills, and perceptions you develop about and around yourself belong to you. Fully portable, they are yours to take with you to a new position, a new employer, a better job, a bigger career. This chapter is about stepping out—*and* stepping up. Even if the reality is that your current job is either going away or gone, you don't have to limit yourself to finding something roughly equivalent to the job you are leaving. When you look beyond your current job, you don't have to look down at your feet or level with the horizon. Why not try looking up?

Potential Employers:
Start Filling Your Prospect Pool

If your overriding aim is to find a new job quickly, you probably won't start by thinking about a new career. Instead, you'll begin by measuring the employer pool your current career offers. Suppose you're in retailing. There are perhaps thousands of firms into which you might move. Of course, the more specialized your area of retailing expertise, the smaller that universe becomes—but also the smaller the pool of those competing with you for employment. As well, if you work in an industry that is concentrated in a given city, say, meat packing in Omaha or publishing in New York, slipping into a new slot is easier than if changing jobs means moving from Chicago to Osaka.

Online Resources

Depending on the size of your industry and how well you know your business, it may be a very simple matter for you to draw up a list of companies similar to the one you have left or are likely to leave. If you've been diligently doing your networking, you may even have some contacts already in mind. If not, now is the time to start searching the relevant print and online publications that feature jobs in your professional field and geographical area. Don't just look for job postings. Also search out news and articles devoted to specific companies and industry issues. These are good sources of hot firms, solid opportunities, trends, and growth areas within your industry. Look for names of article authors (if they are industry professionals) as well as the names mentioned in the articles. Both of these are potential job contacts. Also look for news about promotions, executive moves, retirements, and, yes, deaths. These help you identify possible management-level openings at specific companies.

Think of industry publications as what they are: *interactive*. Instead of just reading them, think about becoming a contributor yourself by writing an article, submitting a news item, or even writing a letter to the editor. Getting published or even quoted in a trade periodical gives you instant credibility and broadcasts your name throughout the industry.

Of course, you should not neglect websites for job seekers. Make sure you monitor and post your résumé on sites devoted to your industry, but also check out the major general-interest megasites. The top 10 (in random order) are:

- Yahoo! HotJobs (http://hotjobs.com)

- JobCentral.com

- CollegeRecruiter.com

- CareerBuilder.com

- Monster.com

- JobFox.com

- Indeed.com

- SimplyHired.com

- Jobing.com

- Net-Temps.com

There is one important caution to observe when using websites for job seekers: *Do* not *post your résumé if you are currently employed—especially if you want to hold on to your job!* These sites are used by those seeking a job as well as those seeking to hire. That's their reason for existence. This means that someone in your current company, maybe even your boss, may well have occasion to surf any number of these sites. Do you want that person to stumble across *your* résumé? No way. It could do you serious damage, and even if you don't like your current job, it's probably better than no job at all.

Seek Professional Help

Despite the abundance of do-it-yourself online employment resources now available, also consider working with an employment agency or a headhunter, especially one who specializes in your industry. You should be aware that most *general* employment agencies are fairly inefficient at connecting you with a job and are rarely helpful at the higher levels of employment. But many companies in search of specialized personnel do make use of industry-specific placement firms or specialized departments of larger executive recruitment firms. Identify the relevant agencies in your field. Google is a good place to start. Many trade associations publish industry directories listing names and numbers of various services useful to the industry.

There are three kinds of agencies available to you:

1. **Permanent employment agencies.** The prospective employer pays the fee (and you pay nothing).

2. **Headhunters.** These are search firms that an employer retains to fill a specific position. As with the employment agency, you pay no fee.

3. **Permanent employment agencies you pay for.** In the first two cases, the agency or headhunter works for the employer, not you. In this case, *you* are the agency's client.

For most people who are changing companies within an industry or career field, the first two options are the most effective and certainly the least expensive.

Do not waste time sending a résumé to an agency or a headhunter. If the agency or headhunter invites letters and résumés online, make use of this portal, but also telephone the agency and bid for a face-to-face interview.

Time for a Change?

After five years as credit manager at Acme Inc., you're ready to move on. Your first thought is to look for credit manager slots at ABC Inc., XYZ Inc., and so on. There are good and obvious reasons for doing this. For one thing, maybe you just love this line of work. For another, it is almost always easier to move from one job to another within the same field than it is to change job descriptions, let alone change careers.

Less obvious but just as compelling are the reasons for making a *big* change, for moving from one career to another. Depending on the size and scope of your industry, the opportunities it offers, and your enduring interest in it, you could spend your entire working life happily moving from one essentially similar position to another within a given industry. But what happens if you get tired of being a credit manager? Or what happens if all the credit manager jobs are taken or otherwise unavailable? Your own heart or the economy my push you to change careers, either by transitioning from a career in one industry to a career in another (from credit manager to high school physics teacher, say) or, less radically, by moving to a new career within your current industry, maybe even within your current company (from publishing house credit manager to book editor).

This second kind of move makes the prospect of career changing less daunting, especially since, in recent years, the corporate landscape of America has been transformed by vertical integration, so that, for example, activities as apparently diverse as book publishing, television production and broadcasting, moviemaking, and digital media production might be seen as the businesses not of three or four separate industries, but, rather, one "media industry." In fact, all of these activities might even be business lines of a single "media company." More than ever before, it is now possible for many of us to change careers *without* leaving our current company. In a troubled time, therefore, you may need to *think* outside of the box without actually having to *walk* outside of it.

Be a Surfer

When television was king of all electronic information/entertainment media, viewers quickly learned to surf channels. Why stick with a program that didn't interest you? After a few minutes—or a few seconds—you clicked over to something else. Now that digital media has pushed television off its throne, web surfing has become the sport of choice, and the few seconds between one channel and the next have been reduced to milliseconds and a mouse click.

Maybe it's time to translate the surfing attitude from TV and the web to what you do for a living. If your job has ended, looks to be in danger of ending, or just seems to you a dead end, the problem might not be this particular job, but the very market, field, or industry that spawned the job in the first place. Those lifelong typewriter repairmen who looked at the IBM PC when it was released in 1981 and decided to retrain for an emerging technology were a lot better off just five years down the road than those who stubbornly stuck with what they already knew. Traditionally, for many, perhaps most, career changers, the reasons for change have been mostly personal:

- They were bored.

- They wanted more money.

- They wanted more of a challenge.

- They woke up one morning, asked "Is this really what I want to do for the rest of my life?" and answered *no*.

- They got tired of popping antacid tablets.

- They now wanted a *less* demanding career, one that left more time for family and other pursuits.

These days, the more pressing reason for changing careers is that *your* career changes out from under *you*. Evolving technology, outsourcing, a contracting economy—all of these might be clear indications that your current career is approaching a dead end. The number of places to move within your field are dwindling.

Once you decide for whatever reason to change careers, start surfing the sea of possibilities. Here's how:

1. Ask and answer: What interests you? Better yet, what *fascinates* you?

2. Seek out people who already do what you believe you may be interested in doing. Ask them about the job. The questions are up to you, but they should include three essentials: *What do you love about your work? What do you hate about your work? How did you get into your work?*

3. Start with what you *want* to do, not with what's "hot" or "in demand." Only after you decide what you want should you set about figuring out if the demand is sufficient to allow you to act on your dream.

4. Start from your transferable skills. If these are a good fit with the prospective career that most appeals to you, your chances of successfully making the change greatly improve.

5. Be proactive. The best time to think about a new career is while you still are being paid in your old one. Career changing tends to demand

time for education and training. If your career change is motivated by the loss of a job, consider taking temporary or part-time work to sustain you while you prepare for your new career.

A Matter of Time and Resources

Time can be an enemy or an ally. It is an enemy when the clock runs on but your bank account runs out. It can be an ally when you realize that a career change does not have to be accomplished in a single leap. You can break down any career (any job, really) into nine parts:

1. Where you work: office, store, farm, etc.

2. Career or job goal(s): to teach math, to repair air conditioners, to sell widgets, and so on.

3. Assigned tasks: for the widget sales rep—become familiar with Acme's line of widgets; identify and target potential customers; contact potential customers; sell (persuade) potential customers; provide requested information; close the sale; transmit the customer's order to the warehouse; follow up with the customer to ensure satisfaction.

4. Tools of the trade: for the widget sales rep—a telephone, a personal computer, an email account, contact-management software, samples and sample case, attractive wardrobe, automobile, and so on.

5. Salary: including commissions, bonuses, and expense account.

6. Time requirement: hours per week, availability after regular business hours, travel time, and so on.

7. Talents and/or traits required: for the widget sales rep—ability to think on your feet, a "people" knack, a good memory, a pleasant telephone voice, a competitive spirit, and a "can-do" attitude.

8. Skills required: for the widget sales rep—ability to persuade people to buy, organizational skills.

9. Knowledge required: for the widget sales rep—familiarity with widget technology and advances in the widget industry; computer savvy.

Break down any prospective career into these constituent parts, and you will realize that even a radical career change rarely calls for changing all of the parts. Typically, the core of a career change requires changing two to three constituents only. Almost always, you will need to acquire new skills and new knowledge. You may also have to call upon talents or traits your old career did not tap into.

Once you determine what new skills and knowledge you will need, ask yourself:

- Can I acquire them?

- Am I willing to invest the time and effort needed to acquire them?

- Do the necessary new skills and knowledge require me to draw on a new set of talents or traits? If so, do I possess them? (If you have no facility with numbers, you probably will not do well as an actuary.)

Estimate the Leap Gap

After you have broken down the prospective career into its constituents, decided what new skills and knowledge you will need to acquire, and given thought to the feasibility of acquiring them, make an estimate of just how far you are going to have to leap to make the transition.

Next, examine your current job title and your current field. The two form a unit that concisely describes your present career. Attempting to move, in a single jump, to a career both with a new job title and in a new field is like trying to swallow a foot-long sandwich in a single gulp. You'll probably choke, and even if you don't, you're not likely to enjoy the meal. Far more feasible is breaking the career change into at least a two-stage process, in which you begin by changing *either* the title *or* the field in order to take a job. Then, after some experience in this job, you make another career move, which completes the transition by changing the component you did not change in step one.

For example: You *are* a sales rep for a book publisher. You *want to be* an advertising copywriter for a maker of computer games. You change your *job title* without leaving the publishing *field*; you find a position in your current company as an advertising copywriter. You work at this for a number of years. Then you also change your *field* by becoming an advertising copywriter for a maker of computer games. Or you do it this way: You leave the publishing company (change your *field*) to become a sales rep for a maker of computer games (keep the same *job title*). Later, you make the transition from the Sales Department to the Advertising Department (you change your *job title*). The first career move, which changes only the job title, may be easier to make without leaving your current company. However, based on your experience in publishing, it is possible to move to a *new* publishing company in a *new* position. The same is true of the second transition. You might move from the sales department to the advertising department in your present company, or find another employer in your field who will hire you not as a sales rep, but as a copywriter.

Back to School?

Changing careers does not always require going back to school, especially if you can manage to make the transition in stages. But many new careers do require new training, and some call for formal schooling. Education is a wonderful thing. The downside is that it takes time and money, and although some careers *require* a certain academic degree, certificate, or number of classroom hours, getting these things does not *guarantee* you a job.

Seek out positions with firms willing to finance your professional training. This may require you to take a lower salary than what you currently have—or had—but weigh this sacrifice against future advances.

Making It Happen

Having thought about what goes into changing careers, it is time to transform the urge to make the change into an actual move. If you are out of a job or almost out of a job, a sense of desperation will likely drive you to rush into something, anything. That's fine. If you need money fast, go ahead and rush headlong into a new job—even one you don't much like. What you should not rush into under any circumstances, however, is a new career. You may *feel* like making a big change. Fine. Addressing your immediate subsistence needs does not obligate you to give up on making that change. In fact, it should put you in a better position for making it.

Don't Seek a Career, Seek Information

Having addressed immediate needs in order to remove or at least lessen the desperation factor, invest time not in a job hunt, but in a knowledge hunt. Seek out an informational interview.

Identify a potential new career, then identify people to talk with about it. Suppose you are interested in getting into reporting business news. Begin by identifying the companies that are producing business news. Next, examine and evaluate their "product." From this evaluation, select the product that most appeals to you: let's say, business news copywriting for the web. Now identify the people who produce the product. Who is writing your favorite Internet business news stories? Make a list. Contact these people.

Send emails or make phone calls. Explain to each person you contact just what you are about.

Of course, this requires that *you* understand what you are about. And that means first understanding what you are *not* about.

- You are *not about* applying for a job.

Should a contact reply to your query by asking you if you are applying for a job, resist the temptation to snap at the bait. Explain that although you are not looking for a job "at the moment," you are "very interested in exploring careers in [whatever the target industry is], and I would be grateful for a few minutes to talk to you about it."

Present your request: "My name is So-and-so. I am very interested in [your industry]. I'm not looking for an immediate job, but I am thinking about a career in [your industry]. It would help me very much if I could spend a few minutes with you, getting your take on [your industry]."

Depending on logistics, try to arrange a face-to-face meeting. But a phone conversation, a video conference (via Skype or other technology), or even an exchange of SMS or other instant messages is far better than nothing.

At minimum, you need to ask:

- How did you get started in this line of work?

- What do you like most about it?

- What do you dislike most about it?

- What are your views on the present state and future prospects of the industry?

- Can you recommend anyone else I might speak with?

Follow your interviewee's lead. If she extends the conversation, great; otherwise, don't let it go on for more than ten minutes or so. Follow up with a thank-you email. Not only is this the right thing to do—you've been given the gift of a busy person's time—it will set your name in the memory of the interviewee and may even get filed away for future reference. Conduct more than a few informational interviews followed up by such emails, and you will soon find that you have broadcast your name to any number of potential employers in a particular industry—*before* you have even begun applying for jobs.

Where the Jobs Are and Will Be

Supplement your informational interviews with some solo research. Do Internet searches on your target industry as well as all the prominent firms in the industry of interest to you. Always examine company websites, with emphasis on press releases and annual reports. Look for recent news stories about the industry, field, and individual companies. Be sure to look at the U.S. Bureau of Labor Statistics website (www.bls.gov) and especially the *Occupational Outlook Handbook*, which the BLS publishes every two years and which is available online. It features up-to-date projections of long-term job growth and employment prospects for nearly three hundred occupations.

It is usually a bad idea to attempt a career change based first and foremost, let alone exclusively, on what's hot now or predicted to become hot in the future. Making yourself indispensable to an organization requires a substantial investment of time and energy. It's well worth it, provided that the organization isn't hot today and gone tomorrow.

As already mentioned, the place to begin is with what interests you and what makes a good fit with your transferable skill set. This said, it will do you little good to pine for a career in an industry with few jobs and dim prospects for future growth. Even if you manage to get a job, once you are in an industry that offers relatively few possibilities, your mobility is limited, and you cannot meet unexpected contingencies as readily as you might in a career path with more branches.

If putting in the hard work to make yourself indispensable is a significant investment, identifying careers in a growth industry is a lot like investing money in growth stocks. In searching for a place to invest your career, emulate the savvy stock market investor who identifies companies whose stocks are currently undervalued, but which are likely to increase dramatically in value. Such investors do not lavish large sums on companies that have already grown—"mature" firms in "mature" markets. Although such blue-chip companies may have a relatively limited downside, their upside is also constrained. In much the same way, you may find more career potential in a growth industry than in a mature industry.

There is no silver bullet for identifying the growth industries. Do the research. Look for current articles on cutting-edge industries. Pick up the "buzz" by doing a web search and counting the number of pages, articles, blogs, and so on devoted to a particular industry during the most recent six-month period.

Let your web search lead you. Suppose you are led to a particular product associated with your target career or industry. Investigate the product. If it's sold at retail, go to the store and ask the salesperson about it. If it's available online, look for customer reviews.

Start reading the stock quotation pages online or in your daily newspaper. Look for companies with a pattern of upward movement in stock prices. Generally speaking, such a pattern suggests that a company is in a growth area—especially if the company is technology oriented or deals in an advanced service.

Easing Into It

Even if you *have* to make a move sooner rather than later, you still have alternatives to sheer desperation. Instead of trying to jump into a new career with both feet, find a way to dip a toe.

If your prospective new career requires going back to school, you have a built-in toe-dipping opportunity. If possible, attend some classes while you are employed. Your classroom experience should give you a useful preview of many aspects of your target career. It is possible that the most valuable thing you'll learn is that the career you thought would be great is just not right for you at all. Better to find out in the classroom instead of the office.

Freelance, Volunteer, Be an Intern

If you already have the training to work in a new career area, consider taking on freelance assignments in that area. Supplement your full-time income by working around your present job. If paid freelance work is unavailable, seek volunteer assignments or even a part-time internship. Identify someone at a company in your target industry who has the power to hire volunteers and interns. Explain exactly what you are thinking: that you are contemplating a move into a career in so-and-so and that you would like to see firsthand how an industry leader operates. You should outline your present position, putting emphasis on the transferable skills that you will, on an unpaid basis, put at the service of the target company. Make it clear that you are *not* looking for a job offer, but that you are seeking experience.

Find a New Place in the Immediate Family

As already noted, you may be able to ease into a new career without even changing companies. You may actually find remarkably little resistance to your proposed career shift, especially in large organizations trying to make the best use of their human capital in challenging times. Find out if your company has special programs in place for career changers. Check them out. If not, identify the leaders in the area of your company to which you would like to move. Talk to them. Seek their advice and support.

Find a New Place in the Extended Family

If you cannot change careers within your present company, explore the possibilities of a new career in a different target company within your present industry. This may take the form of the two-step career transition we discussed. You are presently an accountant working for Acme Widgets. You want to get into sales. You find a job in sales at Beta Widgets. Same industry (widgets), different company, different job title. If you keep your career move within the industry in which you have already built a track record, the transition is likely to be easier for you, and, certainly, you will meet with less resistance from the target employer.

The Future Takes Time

Understand that the future, like any investment, takes time to pay off. Do what you have to do to buy the time, but understand that you can rise, even when you hadn't intended to or don't even want to. A door that closed or is closing on your current job can show you a door to something better, a door that you would never even have looked for, let alone opened, on your own, if circumstances hadn't forced your hand. Find your passion, struggle (if necessary) to maintain your passion, and follow your passion, but also *channel* your passion by guiding it toward a career that offers:

- Adequate income.

- Security, including the potential for growth (a promising outlook).

- A *physical* working environment you can tolerate or even enjoy (outdoors, indoors, busy office, solo home office, and so on).

- An *emotional* working environment you can tolerate or even enjoy (competitive pressures, performance pressures, emotional effect of job hazards, daily stress).

- Acceptable demands on your time (hours per day and per week, holidays and vacation time, deadline pressures, workload).

- People you can work with (kinds of clients or customers, kinds of coworkers, kinds of supervisors, kinds of subordinates).

- Acceptable travel requirements (depending on what you want, travel is a demand or an opportunity).

- Perks and amenities (corner office with a view, company car, company plane, vacation condo, free samples of products, discounts on desirable items).

- Status (how the world values or fails to value the career).

Whether change is your choice or is a necessity thrust upon you, embrace it. If you can be passionate about what you do, you will be driven to make yourself indispensable in whatever you do.

INDEX

Branding yourself *(cont.)*
  high-value brand, 123–25,
    173–74
  low maintenance employees
    and, 112–13
  meaning of, 107–8
  "new" in, 108–10
  popularity in, 120–23
  positivity as, 118–20
  problem solving in, 110–13
  team players and, 177–78
  working more as, 123–25, 127
  your defense of, 128–31
Building new markets
  dream job and, 57
  job satisfaction and, 57
  for marketing yourself, 56–60
  need for, 57
  opportunities in, 56–60
  ownership and, 57
  reasons for, 57
Bureau of Labor Statistics, U.S.,
    209
Burn-out, 179–80
Bush, George W., 177
Business closure signs, 4–6
Business environment
  ethics and, 175–77
  "hostile work environment," 72
  karma and, 66–68
  office space and, 74–76
  rapport and, 65–66
Business ethics, 177
  pilfering and, 175–76

Careers
  compared to jobs, 26–27, 35,
    207
  information for, 204–5
  lateral moves and, 59–60
Career building
  building in, 56–57
  from current job, 57
Career change
  within company, 201–2, 206
  education for, 206–7, 211
  within field, 206
  industry/marketplace
    assessment for, 209–10
  job search for, 201–7
  mechanics of, 203–4
  questions for, 203
  reasons for, 202–3
Career change transition
  within company, 212
  freelance in, 211

  within industry, 212
  intern in, 211
  passion and, 212–13
  single jump in, 205–6
  timing and, 212–13
  two-stage process for, 206
  volunteering in, 211
Career search
  growth industries and, 209–11
  information search vs., 207–9
  for where jobs are, 209–11
Cash flow, in public company, 6
Celebration, 194. *See also*
    Commemoration
  help for, 87
  policies and, 87
  rapport and, 86–87
  routines and, 87
Chairs, 75
Cleanliness, 76
Commemoration
  help in, 88
  rapport and, 87–88
Communication. *See also* Discus-
    sion with boss; Speaking
  company troubles signs and, 6
  in emails, 129
  silence compared to, 6
  in transferable people skills
    inventory, 29–30
Company information
  anxiety from, 16–17
  company stock performance for,
    10, 210–11
  company website for, 9
  for discussion with boss, 8–11
  industry information for, 10–11
  industry publications for, 9–10
  for job interview, 8
  keyword web search for, 9
  memos/newsletters for, 8
  opportunities from, 16–17
  performance evaluations as, 9
  position fit and, 16–17
  results of, 16–17
  sales figures for, 9–10
  web search for, 9
  your job description as, 9
Company merger/sale, 7
Company stock performance, 10,
    210–11
Company strategies, 5
Company troubles sign(s)
  back-benchers and, 4–5
  bad hires as, 4–5
  cash flow and, 6

  communication and, 6
  company strategies and, 5
  layoffs as, 5–6
  market leading and, 5
  quiting as, 4
  star players leaving as, 4–5
  targets and, 5
Company website, 9
Competition
  economy and, 3
  market leading and, 5
  in positioning, 53
Compliments
  modesty and, 148
  as opportunities, 147–48
  replies to, 148–49
Conflict(s)
  in achievement exercise, 45,
    46–47
  compared to friction, 93
  from conflicting goals/needs/
    wants, 95
  in crises, 94
  defensiveness and, 97–98
  destruction from, 94–95
  empathy and, 84
  learning to value, 95–96
  listening and, 97–98
  meaning of, 92
  office diplomat and, 91
  from personal differences, 94
  rapport and, 83–84
  roots of, 93–96
  within self, 93–94
  in situations with a lot at stake,
    94
  usefulness of, 94–96
Conflict management
  action plan for, 104–5
  coach vs. referee for, 96–97
  exercises in, 96–97, 99
  exploit agreement for, 105
  follow through for, 105
  office diplomats and, 93
  Three Musketeer Solution in,
    103–5
  transform disagreement for,
    105
Conflict management
    procedure(s), 98
  ambushes and, 101
  being specific as, 102–3
  choosing battles carefully as,
    100–101
  labeling as, 99
  listening as, 103

multitasking as, 101–2
Conflict resolution, 155, 166
  bullies in, 156–59
  chronic complainers in, 160–61
  passive aggressors in, 159–60
  poachers in, 164–65
  schemers in, 162–64
Creative austerity, 127
Creativity, 27
Credibility, 141–42
Credit
  giving/taking, 121–22, 164–65, 182
  not sharing, 181
  poachers of, 164–65
Criticism
  accepting, 81–82
  alternatives and, 80
  body language and, 82
  from boss, 144–45
  chronic complainers and, 160–61
  consequences of, 81
  gratitude for, 81–82
  job creation and, 60
  language for, 80
  listening and, 82
  offer of mastery and, 20
  permission for, 80
  positive feedback with, 81
  praise and, 80
  rapport and, 79–82
  reality check before, 79–80
  as recognition, 81
  recruiting and, 174
  responses to, 81–82
  serial, 80
  specifics in, 80
  time/place for, 80
  tone/language for, 80
Cubicle etiquette, 74–75
Customers
  creating, sales compared to, 21–22, 68
  external/internal, 51, 114–15, 133
Customer satisfaction. *See also* Boss as satisfied customer
  asking questions for, 116
  for branding yourself as indispensable, 114–18
  creating, 51–55
  customer's mistakes and, 117–18
  extra mile service for, 116–17
  follow-up behavior for, 115

internal/external customers and, 114–16, 133
  marketing yourself for, 52–55

Data, in transferable skills inventory, 25, 27–28, 30–32
Deaths, 87–88
Dedication, 123
Demand contracting, 5–6
Discussion with boss. *See also* Marketing yourself
  achievement exercise for, 45–49
  boss as satisfied customer in, 21–22
  company information for, 8–11
  employment landscape check before, 11–12
  industry/marketplace assessment before, 10–11
  for information, 7–8
  as job interview, 8
  longterm and, 21–22
  offer of mastery in, 18–20
  preparation for, 8–11, 21–22
  self-knowledge before, 12
  transferable skills in, 18
  writing for, 14–18
Downsizing, signs of, 4–6
Dreams, wild, 37–38
Dress/grooming, 72
Dumas, Alexandre, 103
Dunbar, Robin, 190
Durocher, Leo, 66

Economy, competition and, 3
Education, 206–7, 211
Egomania, 121
Emotions. *See* Empathy; Feelings
Empathy, 162
  boss as satisfied customer and, 141–42
  rapport and, 67–68
  selling and, 67–68
  workplace friction/conflict and, 84
Employee development
  ambitions for, 37
  bold offense for, 36–41
  boss for, 21–22, 35–36
  connecting to power for, 38–41, 173
  isolation vs., 172–75
  job postings for, 36
  lateral moves and, 59–60
  office diplomacy and, 91
  office grapevine for, 36–37

problem solving for, 38
  pursuing leads for, 36–37
  structure for, 36
  wild dreams for, 37–38
Employment landscape check
  for better job, 11
  before discussion with boss, 11–12
  for employment market assessment, 11
  before layoff, 11–12
  networking and, 11–12
Ethics, 175–77
Exclusionary behavior
  disrespect as, 73
  ethics and, 175–77
  habitual tardiness as, 72
  inappropriate dress/grooming as, 72
  inappropriate greetings as, 72–73
  inappropriate language as, 71–72
  intruding as, 73
  listening failures as, 73
  poor telephone/email manners as, 72
  rapport wrecking and, 71–73
Exercises
  achievement exercise, 45–49
  achievements inventory, 14–16
  in conflict management, 96–97, 99
  job satisfaction exercise, 50–51
  pre-launch checklist, 55–56
  on problem solving, 45–48
  transferable data skills inventory, 30–32
  transferable people skills inventory, 29–30, 34
  transferable things skills inventory, 32–33
Expense accounts, padding, 176
External customers, 51, 114–15, 133
Eye contact, 138

Feature
  benefit vs., 54–55
  transferable skills as, 54
Federal Express, 54
Feelings, 136. *See also* Conflict resolution; Empathy
  creation of right feelings, 73–76
  greetings and, 74
  issues vs., 99

Layoff(s)
assignments and, 7
being out of the loop and, 7
boss loss and, 6
company merger/sale and, 7
as company troubles sign, 5–6
demand contracting and, 5–6
employment landscape check
before, 11–12
job search before, 11–12
mass layoff, 4–6
new bosses and, 6
offense vs. defense against, 35
office space and, 7
paper trail and, 7
want ads before, 11–12
Leaders, 141–42
Learning, 128
for career change, 206–7, 211
to value conflict, 95–96
LinkedIn, 12, 190–91
Listening, 70
as conflict management
procedure, 103
conflicts and, 97–98
criticism and, 82
failures in, 73
Loyalty, 123

Machiavelli, Niccolò, 162
Madoff, Bernie, 175
Marketing yourself
benefit vs. feature in, 54–55
to boss, 52–56
building new markets for, 56–60
for customer satisfaction, 52–55
job creation and, 58–59
positioning in, 52–55
pre-launch checklist for, 55–56
word of mouth and, 52
Market leading
company troubles signs and, 5
competition and, 5
Mass layoff, 4–6
McFeely, William S., 24
Memos, for company information, 8
Mentor, 29–30, 122
boss as, 39
criteria for, 39
flattery for, 39
offerings for, 39–41
Money. See also Salary
achievements inventory and,
15–16

benefit vs. feature for, 54–55
bottom-line brand, 125–27
creative austerity and, 127
language of business and, 14
mining new sources of, 126
nouns/verbs and, 15–16
offer of mastery and, 19
promotion and, 40–41
self-knowledge and, 14
transferable skills levels and, 27
Monster Networking, 12
MySpace, 190

National Employment Matrix, 107
Negotiating. See also Conflict
resolution
as benefit, 55
for promotion, 152–53
of "routine" salary review,
150–52
in transferable people skills
inventory, 30, 34
Networking, 122, 167, 172
age and, 109–10
being friends as, 185–86
being prepared for, 189
breaking the ice and, 188
employment landscape check
and, 11–12
getting out there as, 186
hazards and, 182
on the job, 183–84, 193–95
LinkedIn/Xing for, 12, 190–91
making/remaking friends and,
174–75
mingling as, 187–88
MySpace for, 190
online resources for, 12
professional organizations/
groups for, 11–12
social inventory for, 186
social media for, 189–93
starting, 184–86
Twitter, 191–93
websites for, 12
Newsletters, 8
Newton, Isaac, 65–66

Occupational Outlook Handbook,
209
Offer of mastery
converting negatives in, 20
criticism and, 20
in discussion with boss, 18–20
money and, 19

negative inventory and, 19–20
specifics in, 19
"Office diplomacy," 63, 91. See
also Conflict management;
Office space
Office grapevine
attention to, 36
being proactive in, 36–37
for employee development,
36–37
specifics for, 37
Office politics, 63, 91
Office romance, 130–31
Office space
assertiveness and, 76
business environment and, 74–76
chairs and, 75
cleanliness and, 76
cubicle etiquette and, 74–75
feelings and, 74–76
identity and, 75–76
layoffs and, 7
office policy and, 76
personalizing, 76
rapport and, 74–76
respect and, 74–75
status and, 75
Online resources, 12. See also
Web search
Opportunity(ies)
apologies as, 85
in building new markets, 56–60
for change, 55
from company information,
16–17
compliments as, 147–48
creation of, 56–60
to offer, 139–40
ownership and, 57
with present employer, 43
problems as, 11
repositioning as, 43–49
setting new goals for, 44
in tough times, 3, 41
transferable skills hierarchy for,
26–27
your job description compared
to, 178–79
Ownership
apologies and, 85–86
of job creation, 61–62
opportunities and, 57

Paper trail, layoffs and, 7
Passion, 212–13

Team players, 177–78
Telephone/email manners, 72
Three Musketeer Solution, 103–5
Time/place
  for criticism, 80
  workplace friction/conflict and,
    83, 84
Timing
  of apologies, 85
  boss as satisfied customer and,
    138–39
  career change transition and,
    212–13
  speaking and, 139
Tough times
  job satisfaction and, 49–50
  opportunities in, 3, 41
  promotions in, 152–53
  self-promotion in, 41
  transferable skills and, 50
Traits
  compared to skills, 22, 24–25
  verbs and, 24–25
Transferable data skills inventory
  creating in, 32
  gathering in, 31
  managing in, 31
  sorting in, 31
  transferable skills hierarchy in, 30
Transferable people skills
    inventory
  coaching/mentoring in, 29–30
  following instructions in, 29
  negotiating in, 30, 34
  transferable skills hierarchy
    in, 29
Transferable skills
  achievements inventory and,
    16–18
  in discussion with boss, 18
  evaluation for, 49
  as features, 54
  job satisfaction exercise and,
    50–51
  promotions and, 18
  skills compared to, 17, 22
  tough times and, 50
  for wild dreams, 37–38
  your job description and, 22,
    25–27
Transferable skills hierarchy
  creativity and, 27
  jobs vs. careers and, 26–27

money and, 27
for opportunities, 26–27
in transferable data skills
    inventory, 30
in transferable people skills
    inventory, 29
in transferable things skills
    inventory, 32
value and, 26–27
Transferable skills inventory.
    See also Transferable data
    skills inventory; Transferable
    people skills inventory
  achievement exercise and, 48
  analyzing, 34
  data in, 25, 27–28, 30–32
  elaboration of, 34
  examples of, 28
  forms for, 29–33
  people in, 25, 27–30
  personal strengths in, 27–34
  refinement of, 34
  self-discovery in, 34
  things in, 25, 27–28, 32–33
  writing, 27–34
Transferable things skills
    inventory
  body skills in, 33
  construction work in, 33
  transferable skills hierarchy
    in, 32
  working with living things in, 33
  working with machinery/
    vehicles in, 32
  working with materials in, 33
Tribe, 12
Twitter, 191–93

Up-selling, 20

Value
  high-value employees, 123–25,
    173–74
  offering, for promotion, 40–41
  problem solving and, 40–41
  transferable skills levels and,
    26–27
"Value proposition," 1
Verbs
  in achievements inventory, 15
  being, self-knowledge and,
    23–27
  money and, 15–16

productivity and, 23–27
traits and, 24–25
Volunteering, 87
  for assignments, 178–79
  in career change transition, 211

Want ads, 11–12
Web search
  for company information, 9
  for job search, 198–200
  keyword, for industry
    information, 10
  of management, 10
  for networking, 12
"What if" language, 61–62
Word of mouth, 52
Workplace friction/conflict, 93.
    See also Conflict resolution
  actions on, 83–84
  empathy and, 84
  management of, 82–84
  persons and, 83–84
  physical danger and, 84
  rapport and, 83–84
  situations and, 83–84
  time/place and, 83, 84
Writing
  achievements inventory, 14–16
  for discussion with boss, 14–18
  self-knowledge and, 14–18
  transferable skills inventory,
    27–34

Xing, 190

Your job
  only doing, 178–79
  self-knowledge compared to, 13
Your job description
  as company information, 9
  opportunities compared to,
    178–79
  transferable skills and, 22,
    25–27
  transformation of, 25–27

ABOUT THE AUTHOR

Jack Griffin, writer and communications expert, is also the author of *How to Say It at Work* and *How to Say It for First-Time Managers*. He is a consultant to corporations, small businesses, government agencies, cultural institutions, and publishers.

ALSO AVAILABLE IN THE HOW TO SAY IT® SERIES...

HOW TO SAY IT FOR FIRST-TIME MANAGERS	Jack Griffin
HOW TO SAY IT: GRANTWRITING	Deborah S. Koch
HOW TO SAY IT, THIRD EDITION	Rosalie Maggio
HOW TO SAY IT ON YOUR RESUME	Brad Karsh with Courtney Pike
HOW TO SAY IT AT WORK, SECOND EDITION	Jack Griffin
HOW TO SAY IT: MARKETING WITH NEW MEDIA	Lena Claxton and Alison Woo
HOW TO SAY IT TO GET INTO THE COLLEGE OF YOUR CHOICE	Linda Metcalf, Ph.D.
HOW TO SAY IT FOR EXECUTIVES	Phyllis Mindell, Ed.D.
HOW TO SAY IT TO SENIORS	David Solie, M.S., P.A.
HOW TO SAY IT FOR WOMEN	Phyllis Mindell, Ed.D.
HOW TO SAY IT WITH YOUR VOICE	Jeffrey Jacobi

HOW TO SAY IT® POCKET GUIDES

HOW TO SAY IT: DOING BUSINESS IN LATIN AMERICA	Kevin Michael Diran, Ed.D.
HOW TO SAY IT: NEGOTIATING TO WIN	Jim Hennig, Ph.D.
HOW TO SAY IT TO SELL IT	Sue Hershkowitz-Coore
HOW TO SAY IT: JOB INTERVIEWS	Linda Matias
HOW TO SAY IT: PERFORMANCE REVIEWS	Meryl Runion and Janelle Brittain

T17.0410